Happy *Child,*
Happy *Home*

Testimonials for *Happy Child, Happy Home: Conscious Parenting and Creative Discipline*

'It is the most accessible and inspiring book on parenting that I have read for a long time. I would not hesitate to recommend it.'

Carol Liknaitzy (parent of 5, grandparent, early childhood Steiner teacher-training facilitator in Australia and South Africa)

'Today I am more relaxed around my son, and I am able to steer my parenting in the right direction so we are more in harmony with each other. I feel I have more skills to bring out the best in him – thank you for giving me parenting tools for life!'

Carolyn Charlton (parent)

'I recommend Lou's books and website to parents wherever I go.'

Rachel Watt (Founder of Barefoot *magazine and psychologist)*

'What I loved about *Happy Child, Happy Home* is just how simple it is to make changes that result in happier children and parents.'

Josie Connor (parent)

'Lou's first book is my highest-selling parenting book; my customers are already waiting for *Happy Child, Happy Home* to be published.'

Melissa McGroarty (Honeybee Books and Toys, Australia)

'Lou is such a skilled writer and her experience as a mother and a teacher informs every word. There's no 'waffle', just practical, beautiful words of wisdom: highly recommended!'

Emily Donaldson (parent)

Happy *Child,*
Happy *Home*

Conscious Parenting and Creative Discipline

Lou Harvey-Zahra

Floris Books

For Bettye Palmer
who loved children and they loved her

First published in 2014 by Floris Books
Second printing 2014
© 2014 Lou Harvey-Zahra

Photography: Rebecca Landy
Craft photography: Jayson Zahra

Lou Harvey-Zahra has asserted her right under the Copyright Act 1988
to be identified as the Author of this Work

 This book is also available as an eBook

British Library CIP Data available
ISBN 978-178250-055-1
Printed in Great Britain
by DS Smith Print Solutions, Glasgow

Acknowledgements

Thank you to: Ged, for being a wonderful husband and dad; my two children, Jayson and Jessica, for bringing love, laughter, creativity, and noise to our home; my parents, Pam and Michael, for role-modelling unconditional love; Floris, for producing such wonderful and inspiring books - your books have lined my bookcase for decades; Ocea Lynette Goeby (age 6), for drawing such a wonderful front cover for me; Rebecca, for your gift of capturing the purity of childhood; parents, for telling their real life stories; finally to Michael, for your early proofs and words of wisdom as our 'dad's voice'.

To all families who take inspiration from my words, I feel very blessed to share with you.

Contents

Introduction

A hundred years from now it will not matter what my bank balance was, the sort of house I lived in, or the kind of car I drove – but the world may be a different place because I was important in the life of a child.

FOREST E. WITCRAFT

What is 'Conscious Parenting'? Conscious Parenting describes the approach of parents who try to stay open-minded and present with their child's needs and behaviours. Conscious Parenting is the care of children that emerges when we see the world from a child's perspective and understand the important stage of childhood. Children are not little adults; they have their own world, their own way of looking at life. Conscious Parenting asks: What is important in that world? What do I need to provide to truly nurture childhood and create a happy home? Many answers to these questions are found in this book, which is full of suggestions I have practised and insights I have applied in my personal and professional life with children.

In this book we will explore the ways that connection, creativity and communication in family life lay the foundation for a happy childhood and a happy home. I call these keys to happiness 'the three 'C's'. It is these three 'C's working together that leads to the big 'C': consciousness. It is through practising connection, creativity and communication at home that we arrive at conscious parenting.

No microchip is downloaded the moment we become parents. We do not know how to deal with challenging discipline issues, provide positive play spaces or create Christmas craft! *Happy Child, Happy Home* is a parenting guide to take along on the journey. It will support you as you develop the ideas and awareness that foster happy and healthy children and make a house a home. This book aims to cover a very broad range of topics in one easy read. It is for parents to pick up when they seek inspiration, support, information or guidance.

I have witnessed families where the three 'C's were not present; it was evident to me that day-to-day life was a struggle for both parent and child. And, having helped parents discover the three 'C's, I have then watched positive transformations in the family home.

The ideas in *Happy Child, Happy Home* aim to develop calm and happy children who feel connected to their loved ones. Rather than this being hard work for parents, it is a way to joy and makes the parenting journey easier. This book envisages the home as a creative environment that fosters positive behaviours and a strong bond between parent and child.

Happy Child, Happy Home is written in a highly practical way. Note that the title is not 'Perfect Parenting'. I know how hard it can be! I have years of training and experience in caring for children, yet I am not a perfect parent − far from it. I also know that if we were perfect, this would ultimately be difficult for our children: living up to 'perfection' is impossible! Conscious Parenting involves being aware of when things in the family are not working, and being willing to change them. I do strive to become more aware of my shortcomings and make changes (albeit slowly at times).

Family life can be seen as an 'emotional bank account': large withdrawals will happen from time to time. Challenges are inevitable as we go through the years, so we need to put in positive deposits on a daily basis. Investments from stable, happy and connected times see us through patches of disconnection or anger. *Happy Child, Happy Home* is full of practical ideas that can function as deposits in the family's emotional bank account, and stop you from going into the red!

Over the past twenty years I have sought to understand children's developmental needs through my work as a teacher in primary, special needs and Rudolf Steiner settings; as a playgroup leader and parenting workshop facilitator; and of course in parenting my own two children. This book contains much of what I have seen and learnt, but I have also included many other voices, including the real stories of parents who have talked with me, thoughts from a dad's perspective (Michael), and words from my son, Jayson, at the age of seven, so a child can also be heard here.

The thought of writing this book came to me when I was pregnant with my first child. After the birth I was so inspired by parenting and the joys of early childhood I embarked on a fourteen-year quest to explore what might make a happy child, a happy home, a happy Earth. I wrote on bits of paper everywhere I went, and even asked for a dictaphone from Father Christmas to note my inspirations. I tried different activities and approaches, fell down at times, picked myself up, and tried again! I wrote notes because I always wanted to share my tips and discoveries with other parents. This book is the result, and it is one I would have loved as a new parent.

For me, parenting is not about theories — I am far from being an academic; what we need are the practical ideas and approaches that make everyday family life full of love, joy and (where possible!) fun. There are many books about parenting, but for me the essence of it all is building a strong family life. All the parenting tips I have presented are about connecting, communicating and creating together as a family.

A child's pivotal, formative experiences happen within family life. The quality of family life shapes a child's future attitudes, and colours their approach to the world. As parents, we are the creators of our children's experiences; we shape their whole framework for being and understanding. When we are more conscious, we enhance children's potential to become happy, centred and fulfilled adults. While this is a big statement, it is the small, everyday ideas for family life that make the BIG difference. Conscious Parenting is not about doing entirely new or major things with your children; it is the everyday little things that matter.

All the ideas in this book have been tried and tested. They have put smiles on children's faces, created happy hearts, and enhanced the bonds between parents and children. Small changes count. Throughout this book, we discover together how to make ordinary family moments extraordinary. I hope to empower even the least creative parent (really, there's no such thing — have courage!) to become a story-teller and to provide wonderful times of making and doing for their young ones. Children will love you for it! I also explore creative discipline; that is, tools for transforming behaviour in a positive manner.

You might like to write down thoughts and points in a journal while reading this book. This will help ground and reinforce ideas you discover that relate to your family, and assist in putting them into action. Many of the new ideas here take only minutes to try but might lead to long-term change and become part of your happy home.

Chapters One, Two and Three of *Happy Child, Happy Home* are about positive family rhythms. Chapter One is full of suggestions for structuring days with children and making ordinary moments, like mealtimes or bedtimes, a bit extraordinary. Chapter Two gives ideas for celebrating annual festivals like birthdays and Christmas. Chapter Three has activities that will bring us closer to the four seasons.

Chapter Four discusses craft, creativity and easy ways we can make things together with our children. Chapter Five explains the joy of storytelling, and shares ideas that will help parents make up their own tales to delight their young ones. Chapters Six and Seven reinforce the importance of imaginative play in children's lives and discuss ways of supporting play in our homes.

Chapter Eight delves beneath the surface to see how parents can nurture children's twelve senses and so foster health and happiness. Chapter Nine on creative discipline gives practical tools for transforming children's everyday challenging behaviours into positive outcomes. Chapter Ten explains the Four Temperaments, leading to a greater understanding of your children.

And Chapter Eleven contains a checklist of 101 ways you can make your household more environmentally sustainable.

At the end of my days I know the question in my mind will be, 'Did I connect enough to my loved ones?'

Parents have the most important job on the planet: guiding the next generation. Our efforts positively affect the health and happiness of our children and family life, now and for generations to come. Let's aim to keep our minds and hearts wide open (without judging ourselves too harshly!) to consciously observe how our parenting is shaping our children and the Earth. This is a lifetime journey for us all.

Blessings along the road!

Chapter One
Positive Family Rhythms

Stop the glorification of busy!

ANON

The universe has rhythms. Day and night, the seasons of the year, and high and low tides are examples of the perfectly balanced rhythms of our planet. We have rhythms inside us: our heartbeat, our breathing and our walking pace.

Positive family rhythms — daily, weekly and yearly routines and rituals — provide a foundation of stability, trust, love and connection for a household. This foundation leads to happier, more settled children. Family rhythms help to keep life in balance, and children love them!

Are You Leading a Hurried Life?

I heard parenting author Steve Biddulph talking about the book he wrote with his wife, Sharon, *The Complete Secrets of Happy Children* (Thorsons), and a comment he made then has stayed with me: 75 per cent of discipline and behavioural problems are caused by the hurry that parents are in. How rushed are we, and how rushed are we making our children? Faster is not necessarily better! It is harder to connect with each other when going at great speed. It's good to slow down, look into our children's eyes, observe what is happening around us and smell the roses. And let our children smell them too!

As children grow, they want to do more on their own. It requires time and patience to allow them to do up their own buttons or shoelaces. Rushing out of the door does not give children the time to accomplish what they want and need to do for themselves and for their development. Nor does it give them time to truly play and relax (we discuss the importance of imaginary play later). Overstimulated, tired and hurried children can be very grumpy. (As can adults, too!)

Let's spend a day being less busy. In this chapter I suggest putting a day into your weekly routine when the family can take life slowly. You'll be surprised at what a difference even one day makes.

Because having to go faster is sometimes a fact of life, there are also tips for 'happy hurrying' at the end of the chapter. At other times, we parents have to remember to slow down and enjoy the gentle, quiet rhythm of the day, so we can give this gift to our children. Let's take a deep breath...

Healthy Rhythms — Breathing In and Out

Think of the day as a series of in-and-out breaths. We fill our days with activities; some of these are classed as breathing-in activities, involving slowing-down periods and quiet play at home, being peaceful. Children need time to connect and re-centre during the day. This might be done with a meal or snack, indoor imaginative play, quietly helping with chores, a rest time in a comfortable area, stories on the couch or big bed, a cuddle on the knee with songs, or a shared peaceful bath. Breathing-in activities allow us to connect, slow down and look into each other's eyes. Breathing-out activities are more active: outings, social gatherings, big and noisy play, outside play, perhaps more structured activities inside and outside the home.

If children's play and behaviour becomes disruptive or loses its momentum, offer an in-breath activity. Allow children time to centre again, connect to loved ones and refuel, before sending them back out into the busy world. Imagine this breathing-in-and-out rhythm occurring in your home throughout the day. It can help to give you a sense of a nurturing pattern that is keeping you and the children in sync.

Children who go from one breathing-out activity to the next can become quite demanding for entertainment. 'What are we doing today?' 'What are we doing next?' 'Where are we going?' You may then hear the words, 'I'm bored', because they are so used to being entertained. Children require quiet spaces in each day to create play from within. They need time to be imaginative, to play quietly, be nurtured and spend rest periods with loved ones.

Out in the morning? Try staying at home in the afternoon, and vice versa. This brings balance to the day. If we have a busy social day out, can we stay at home the next day?

Every family has different work commitments and different quantities of time they can spend at home. Remember, however, that as parents it is we who hold the key for creating positive and balanced rhythms for our children. Children will go, go and go. And then have a meltdown!

Adults also benefit greatly from periods of breathing in. We too easily forget to rest ourselves. Adults have been known to throw tantrums, too, from being too busy. (I know!) Being a constantly busy parent has consequences in family life. When I make unwise parenting choices, I am usually stressed about something else or rushed.

At the end of each day, reflect, 'Did we breathe in today? Can we keep life in balance, to allow our children to be balanced?'

The Concept of Time

Young children do not understand concepts of time such as one o'clock, ten minutes, two days, Monday or Friday. A child's time zone is NOW. I reassured an anxious child during school playtime that I would be back in five minutes. Her response: 'I don't know what five minutes means!' Young children have an understanding of time that comes from the rhythm of their lives. What can make sense to them is breakfast time, playtime, afternoon nap time, playgroup day, baking day and pancake Sunday. Maintaining a consistent rhythm to their day – and week – helps children feel nurtured, stable and joyous. They are able to enter into each activity with the knowledge that they can have this experience again and again, and they have the pleasure and reassurance of anticipating future routines and events.

Rhythm does not mean rigidity. Rather, it is a chance to

make little moments special. Family rhythms bring wonderful experiences into our days, weeks and years together. It also ensures that we spend time on the things we most value, rather than on what we assume is most pressing. Building a lovely and considered family rhythm means that the weeks do not go by with the thought, 'I meant to do that, but...'

Let us look at an ordinary day and see what moments parents can make extraordinary for their children. Even if we are 'time poor', most of the suggestions below take half a minute or so, and hold priceless gifts for children, gifts of connection, communication and creativity in daily life. They also hold the key to fewer struggles of wills, and maximise positive behaviours during meals, rest and bedtimes.

Daily Rhythms

Wake Up, It's a New Day!

How do our children wake up? It is beneficial, where possible, for children to wake up by themselves, once they have had enough sleep – to slowly open their eyes, stretch and yawn before getting up and out into the new day. A positive bedtime rhythm (explained later in this chapter), which assists with getting them to sleep at their bedtime, also helps with them being ready for the day the next morning.

How are we to 'meet' children each day? Step into their shoes, and imagine how you would like to be greeted! Like the rising of the sun, create emotional warmth and bonding to start the day together. When my children were younger, on days with no deadlines to rush out for, I would try to stay in bed, so that my little ones could join me for cuddles and love to start the day.

This is a time of butterfly kisses (tickling with your eye lashes on a soft cheek), cuddles, stories and a chat. Many years later, with school times to meet, I still consciously start the day by saying, 'My beautiful, how are you? How was your sleep?' Or I just say 'My darling' and hold them briefly as we meet in the corridor. Five seconds of touch and a few kind words is a great beginning to the morning. The day may get busier, and we may not see much of each other, but we have already experienced a moment of connection.

When children are young, try a little song while opening the curtains (add in your child's name and two of her or his friends):

Good morning sun, how are you today?
It's a new day with lots of time to play.
I wonder will [Name 1] play with [Name 2] or [Name 3] today?

Mealtime Magic

The mealtime table is a special place in our homes: a place to enjoy food, yes, but also a place where the family can bond. Family meals are perfect occasions to connect, create and communicate together.

We have lost touch, in our heavily processed fast-food world, with the idea that our food is slowly grown in the Earth, planted by a farmer, helped along by the warmth of the sun and some lovely wet showers. We can bring back that magical gratitude and connection with each other and the Earth at mealtimes, and we can begin when our children are very young.

What is breakfast like at home? When children are young, and if there is time, it can be fun to sit down together and invite the three bears along to share the porridge. Or have a special milk jug for little hands to pour.

For morning or afternoon tea, create a daily fruit and vegetable 'happy face' plate. Cut fruit and vegetables into pieces that can form a picture. Bananas are great for lips, carrot sticks for hair, sliced apples for ears and so on. Try more adventurous pictures together, a train perhaps? This is a fun and creative daily food rhythm to encourage healthy eating. Share the plate together: 'I will eat an eye now!'

At lunchtime, if you are at home together, sit with your child and play a 'thank you' game: 'Thank you to the farmer who grew the wheat that made the bread that I am eating'; 'Thank you to the cow that gave the milk that made the cheese'; 'Thank you to the clouds and showers that watered the fruit that I am eating'. This not only tells children where their food comes from, it helps them feel part of the larger community and brings gratitude and respect back to the dinner table – valuable qualities we lose in a fast-paced life.

I say this blessing each day at school – it builds a stable and joyous rhythm to daily life:

> Earth who gives to us this food,
> Sun who makes it ripe and good,
> Dear Earth, dear Sun, by you we live,
> Our loving thanks to you we give.

If you feel so inspired, have a candle, a candle snuffer and a little vase for flowers on the family dinner table. These simple things make a significant difference. Children can help to cook, set the table and pick the flowers for the vase. Then when the meal is put on the table, the child feels connected to it and to us.

At meals, sit together as a family whenever you can. The family dinner table is truly a time of communication, as well as nourishment. Each family member takes it in turns to say what their favourite part of the day was, and to share daily news, however simple, with each other. Children as young as two can have a turn. My husband is an accountant – he might say that he got a new client. The news doesn't have to be exciting! Be a role model of communication for children to follow: 'Now, let me see, what was my favourite part of the day, what shall I share with you today?'

If directly asked about their day, children may be reluctant to share. However, if adults naturally act as role models, sharing their days first as a game, children are more likely to take their turn. If not, there is always another dinnertime.

By fostering this daily rhythm of chatting at the dinner table (with the TV kept off!) in the vital years, it continues naturally for life. Yes, perhaps we will have teenagers who communicate with more than a grunt! If one parent works late, the at-home parent can sit with the children during their meal and have a light snack, trusting that the family will eat together at the weekend.

To end the meal, the child can blow out the candle, or extinguish it with the snuffer. If you forget, your child will soon remind you: 'The candle, Mummy!' Candles bring a little bit of magic into children's lives, and such rituals may also keep them sitting at the table for longer! Remember that small children eat regularly – there is a need for breakfast, morning tea, lunch, afternoon tea and dinner in most households. Hungry children are grumpy children. Regular eating and resting helps to create a cheerful day. This means there are many opportunities to eat well and connect together!

If you are out in the day and mealtime cooking is rushed, try cooking double and freezing one meal each time. This can be a lifeline on busy evenings and can calm evening nerves. When my children were young, I would cook in the morning, with their help if interested. This allowed us to be relaxed in the afternoon. Resting the dish through the day added to the taste of the meal!

A Word from a Dad – Michael

To get on well with kids, cook. I recall an aunty making pikelets with me, and this is a special childhood memory. I made bread dough each week when my daughter was young. We made it look like a smile: two rolls for eyes and a sausage shape for a smiley mouth.

A Suggestion

The tastebuds of preschoolers can create tension at mealtimes. Try a smorgasbord-style plate in the middle of the table for the whole family (alongside the meal), that has chopped veggie sticks, slices of cheese, nuts and sunflower seeds on it, to add more vegetables and protein to your children's diet. It's fun to pick our own food.

Relaxing Rest Times

Younger children need a sleep in the afternoon, or, when a little older, a rest. Encouraging a sleep or rest routine helps children's energy levels, health and five o'clock moods! If they say they do not want to rest, lie on your big bed and start reading a story. Pretend to read it to teddy! They will usually be enticed over – they cannot resist. Consistent nurturing and healthy rhythms are vital.

To turn rest time into a happy ritual, maybe have a special sleeping bag just for resting in during the day, a rest-time candle, or a child's sofa where you curl up to have a story with the soft toys? Perhaps fill a special basket with interesting, quiet and calming activities for quieter play – for example, a water bottle filled with water and sparkles can be a mesmerising thing. Buy some new rest-time books, never seen before, and keep them in your special rest-time basket. You could have the basket of toys for quiet play in your bedroom so they can open it while you rest! Perhaps use a timer that rings when rest time is over. A magical den made by throwing a large bed sheet over the kitchen table, and putting cushions and books underneath, cocoons a child for a while. Go in too, and read stories together. Is the weather sunny? Lie together and read under a tree, or watch the leaves dance and find pictures in clouds.

Even when my children went to kindergarten and school, they required some tender loving care at four in the afternoon. This applies to any children coming in from a busy day at kindergarten, preschool or the early school years. As they walked in the door at home, I had a snack ready on the table and I read to them from a chapter book. This short time allowed us all to relax and connect together and helped the rest of the evening go smoothly. But when I came grumbling in the door, and rushed to start chores and to put things away, nerves were often frazzled.

Adults tell me that this point is for them as well: remembering to have a daily rest has enhanced their lives and moods too!

Children who have a nurturing sleep or rest rhythm and healthy regular meals tend to get less niggly and sensitive. Difficult behaviour may often be caused by overtiredness, hunger and dehydration. Also, a lack of connection to loved ones. Resting and going to sleep can be a very precious time to breathe in, and a sacred bonding time in our relationships. Imagine how we, as children, would most like to be put to bed.

Bedtimes to Dream About

A healthy going-to-bed rhythm and consistent bedtime are important for childhood development and happiness. To hear fewer 'no's at sleeptime, incorporate fun and nurturing end-of-the-day rituals into family life. Cutting out all electronic stimuli (TV and electronic games) before bed also helps.

Begin the bedtime rhythm each evening in a creative way: young children enjoy getting a ride to the bathroom standing on a parent's feet (facing the parent and holding onto their legs) or a gentle plane trip on Daddy's shoulders. I have even seen a saddle for dads! 'The horse needs to go to the stable!'

Once in the bathroom, teeth brushing can be made inspiring by playing a little imaginative game. I have not yet known a child who does not like 'teethy tales'. All children are basically egocentric; they like to hear about themselves, so tell a tale about the daily adventures of each tooth as it is cleaned! Name the foods, toys and people that your own child will remember: 'This tooth ate [cornflakes/porridge/toast] for breakfast; this tooth played with [toy cars/Sooty the cat/wooden blocks]; this tooth loved to eat [cheese on toast/an apple/pasta] for lunch; this tooth smiled at [Nannie/Sophie/your sister].' This little game makes teeth cleaning fun, and recounting the special parts of the day is a lovely way for children to finish their activities and wind down for bed. If a child has been at kindergarten or nursery, their daily events can be guessed.

I recently received an email from a mum, thanking me for the idea of teethy tales. She told me that each day she called her partner on his way home from work, and filled him in on the events of the day. At teeth cleaning time, their daughter was always amazed. How did Daddy know about her teeth's adventures?

Another teeth cleaning game is to talk as if you are the tooth: 'Don't forget me, I may be at the back, you left me out, boohoo!' This encourages cleaning each tooth properly.

Giant steps

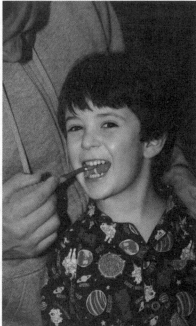

Teethy tales

Bedtime connection

My dentist advised us to clean the children's teeth until they were seven, as young children tend to suck and chew the toothbrush.

Getting from the bathroom to the bedroom can be made fun with a piggyback ride, or marching like the Grand Old Duke of York. Make it enjoyable, but not too stimulating!

Something to Try

Do you need to encourage a boy to go to the toilet as part of the bedtime rhythm? Place a ping-pong ball in the toilet (it will float and not flush away). Now you've turned a boring interruption to his play into an aiming game. Dad can try it too, when no one is looking!

Once in bed, there are many creative ideas to help your young ones move to dreamland. And children will like the same song or routine for nine years; there's no need to keep thinking of new ideas! Say 'goodnight' to three things in the room, followed by a lullaby with nice words, and a soft touch. Remember that young children love to hear their parents sing, regardless of whether we think we can sing or not! Singing yourself is far more powerful and beautiful than playing recorded music. By surrounding our child with our own singing voice and caring touch, we are wrapping them in a sweet blanket of our love. Dads, Elvis Presley is fine – any tune, as long as it's slow and loving. Make this a daily rhythm and see your children go off to sleep with a soft smile! Bedtimes can become a big gift of love for children.

Children tend to enjoy one lullaby in particular. Because he loved trains, my son's favourite was 'Train Whistle Blowing'. He moved to the bedroom after a whistle and toot, toot! My daughter's favourite was 'Moo, Little Cow Moo', because she loves animals. I also told her the bedtime poem called 'Good Night' each night. It can be found in Diana Carey and Judy Large's *Festival, Family and Food* (Hawthorn Press).

No more work and no more play,
Every toy is put away,
Ended is the lovely day,
Then – goodnight!

Drink the milk all white and creamy,
Have your bath all warm and steamy,
Close your eyes all tired and dreamy,
Then – goodnight!

Through the window stars are peeping,
From their holes the mice [I say 'possums'!] are creeping,
Your white bed is soft for sleeping,
Then – goodnight!

Here is a poem I said to my daughter at bedtime, while drawing the star, sun and moon on her back:

Wishing Star

A star for you to wish on,
A sun so warm and bright,
A moon for you to sleep on,
Happy dreams,
A kiss goodnight.

My daughter when younger was always quite restless going to bed, and she would get up with any excuse. But she tended to settle much more easily when she had a ride on Daddy's shoulders to the bathroom, teethy tales, her special bedtime poem and a lullaby while her hair was stroked. One night, when I was in a rush – yes, a hurried life! – I skipped all of her rhythm and just said, 'Go to sleep, it's late!' There was a little voice, 'Mum, have you not worked out that when you sing to me and stroke my hair, I have sweeter dreams?' The wisdom of a six year old!

Touch is important: build it into the bedtime rhythm. It has the power to settle difficult or restless behaviour and allows for a deeper connection.

For many years I used a soft, simple tune to sing about those people that love my daughter – including our animals – while stroking her hair and face. What is given to children, they tend to give back out to the world. I once found my daughter in our lounge and she had wrapped our dog in a blanket. She was stroking his head lovingly while sweetly singing the lullaby to him, remembering to mention all the neighbourhood dogs who loved him! The look on the dog's face was one of pure bliss!

During my parenting workshops, parents share their own unique bedtime rhythms. One family asks their children to 'blow out' the light each night, as they turn the switch. (Magic!) Another family play a bedtime game called 'Thank Your Lucky Stars'. I love it! At bedtime, take it in turns to think of something to be thankful for. Feelings of gratitude help with sleep.

Another example of a loving bedtime rhythm that worked well in our house was needed when my sister came to stay with her two children. She had recently split from their father, and the children were very distressed, particularly at bedtime. They did not want to go to or stay in bed. My sister was finding it harder and harder to cope. We worked together and reinvented the bedtime routine, emphasising fun. In the midst of the tears one night, my husband came in brandishing his long Tai Chi sword. 'All who follow me get to hold my sword!' he announced, and off he went, up the stairs, singing 'Oh, the Grand Old Duke of York'. The six-year-old boy was mesmerised and up he went! At the top of the stairs, we all went marching into the bedroom and took it in turns to hold the mighty sword! Next, we held a special big crystal while sharing our favourite part of the day. We listened and laughed at all the daily memories. We learnt a lullaby together. The evening was fun, we all connected and, yes, they were in bed! Years later, the boy still held a crystal at night, and liked lavender oil on his pillow, to help with going to sleep.

A special night light can be left on to help comfort a child and give a little light to the room. I bought each of my children a stained-glass lamp – a turtle and a butterfly. These special lamps create a lovely soft light and can remain with them, if they're not broken, even when they live on their own and put themselves to bed!

When the lead-up is slow and nurturing, it is much easier for children to wind down and sleep. Watching TV or being highly stimulated can cause behavioural difficulties. Also, many films and electronic games have a scary character, and these can create images that play on a young child's mind and may cause bad dreams. Be conscious of what children are watching and absorbing.

I'll be Back in Five Minutes

When children are very young, it can work well to stay with them as they fall asleep. When ready, start making this time shorter by saying, 'I'm going to wash up, and then I will be straight back in again.' Always give children the promise of returning and the reassurance of fulfilling the promise. Keep repeating this until they are asleep. 'I'll be back to check on you after I've made a cup of tea.'

Something to Try: Taking it in Turns

In our house, when our children were younger, their father and I had a rhythm so we could share putting them to bed. Variations on this rhythm would work in any household where there are two adults caring for the children. For two weeks I put our son to bed and my husband put our daughter to bed, then for the next two weeks we swapped. We began this cycle at the new moon and then swapped at the full moon. The children looked out the window to see which moon it was – to know when it was time for a change. This rhythm meant that we got to have one-on-one time with each child. We enjoyed connecting, and feeling their unique way of being. The children enjoyed both parents putting them to bed and became entirely comfortable with either of us in this role. I wrote out the poem and lullaby for my husband to sing to our daughter, which he gallantly did, and she would giggle, loving having her daddy sing.

When they are older and can understand, if they keep calling you back or getting up, say calmly and softly, 'It is Mummy's special time now; it's time for you to be asleep.' Of course, if they are distressed or crying, stay with them and settle them. If they are just calling out or happily getting up, reinforce that at their bedtime they go to sleep and Mummy or Daddy has some time to her or himself.

My son stopped wanting a lullaby when he was about eight years old. He now has an 'I love you' or kind words whispered in his ear, and a kiss – short and sweet. For years my daughter wanted her simple made-up lullaby mentioning everyone who loves her. Once she was older, she would write one thing in her gratitude diary. To end the day, I now like to lie on my daughter's bed and have a chat instead of a lullaby. Your family will find its own bedtime rituals, and adapt them over time.

A daily rhythm of morning greetings, mealtimes, rest times and bedtimes leads to fewer tantrums and meltdowns. It also builds a sense of stability and belonging, turning ordinary everyday moments into opportunities to connect, create and communicate together.

Great Gratitude

Feeling gratitude floods us with 'the happy hormone': oxytocin. This hormone makes humans feel safe and connected and tells the brain 'everything is alright'.

The two daily gratitude games mentioned above, 'Thank Your Lucky Stars' and the mealtime 'thank you' game, help build gratitude into family life. Gratitude is great for parents too! Feeling good makes us more compassionate and patient parents – at least some of the time!

Being grateful is not ignoring the difficult times; it is recognising what we do have. As parents, we can try building a regular habit of taking a moment to reflect and acknowledge what life has given us – perhaps at night before going to sleep or perhaps when we stop at traffic lights or any other trigger that happens regularly. A practice such as this creates calming hormones and leads to a happier life. We all have something to be grateful for.

Real Life Story
Connie – 'Schlaf, Kindchen, Schlaf'

My seven-year-old son still loves hearing the same
German lullaby we have sung to him since he was a
baby. It's called 'Schlaf, Kindchen, Schlaf'. We snuggle up
together in his bed, and although I have to remind him
what the words mean (as we tend not to speak German),
he loves it so much he doesn't want it replaced by a new
lullaby. It shows how sensitive young children still are at
that age.

Weekly Rhythms: Precious Connection Time

The concept of 'breathing-in-breathing-out' works for rhythms
in the week, too. The world seems to move so fast! This can have
an effect on the connection between parents and their children.
Parents have different work commitments and schedules, but can
a week include one or two days at home?

A 'home day' is when we do not get in a car, but stay at home
or in the garden, and in the local neighbourhood. There are no
time schedules to adhere to. These slower days can become a
sanctuary for parents and children. Time to stay in your pyjamas
for longer, set up big imaginary play scenes, bake and wash up
together, play in the garden and watch a bug, cuddle in bed for a
story at rest time, and enjoy the luxury of bathing together in the
afternoon when everyone else is at work and busy. Make the most
of this unhurried pace of life. By slowing down on some days, we
can really smell the flowers. What a lovely scent!

Does a young child really need so many outings and activities
in one week? Imaginative play at home is the ideal activity for
a growing child. Less is often more. Look at the overall week

and try to balance going-out days with staying-at-home days. Combine this with good play options, craft and cooking ideas (you will find many in later chapters) and you may start to feel that 'home is where the heart is'.

What Day is it Today?

Imagine going to your usual weekly yoga class, and finding a sign on the door saying that it was held the day before, or visiting extended family on Sunday, to be told that the rest of the family was coming on Monday. This is how children feel when there is no consistent weekly rhythm in their life: disorientated, and at times confused!

Create a weekly rhythm around enjoyable family activities. This means that special time together does happen: we have prioritised it and made a regular place in our schedules for it. Some examples of activities that might find a place in your weekly routine include:

* Baking Day – bake together for the biscuit tin;
* Nature Walk Day – pack a little rucksack and walk to the park to see the ducks;
* Pancake Day – make pancakes together on a Sunday morning; or
* Craft Day – paint, or make a special seasonal craft project (see the craft chapter).

At a workshop I ran where we talked about weekly rhythms, a mum said the rest of her week was so busy, her Fridays at home were essential. She always bakes morning tea with her children, to eat on a picnic blanket at home. They pour peppermint tea ceremoniously from a teapot for everyone to share. What family fun!

My first child loved baking and cooking. He was involved with most meals and once a week he baked by himself (with a little assistance!) for the biscuit tin. My daughter loved craft. Once a week, when she was younger, we would make craft together out of an environmental projects book. At present my children love family games night. The whole family sits down to Uno or plays a game of table tennis. Another rhythm, now Jayson is fourteen, is that he goes to lunch with Dad every Saturday. Rhythms are important with older children too, to make sure the family tribe remains strong. Look to the child's interests for inspiration. Why not start a new family rhythm and see how it goes...

I always bathed with my children on Saturday morning, while their daddy had a lie-in. On Sunday morning, it was my turn for a lie-in because Daddy made pancakes with the children. This rhythm has been going on for years and when the answer to 'What day is it tomorrow?' is 'Pancake Day!', this has always been met with smiles and laughs.

Here is the pancake recipe – give it a try!

Pancakes

* 200 g (7 oz) flour
* 500 ml (16 fl oz) milk
* pinch of salt
* cinnamon
* 2 eggs

Combine flour, cinnamon and salt. Make a well and add milk and eggs. Whisk until smooth. Melt a little butter in the frying pan, drop in pancake mix to desired thickness, cook and flip (or turn). Yum!

Treats in a Weekly Rhythm

Rhythms help avoid tantrums! Rhythms are part of creative discipline and they reduce nagging. It can be helpful to put food you want to limit into a weekly rhythm. Friday is always 'Treat Night' in our house. When children ask for something at the supermarket, I remind them that 'Treat Night' is Friday. If you allow TV, put your guidelines about watching it into a healthy rhythm that you are happy with. Stick to this rhythm: children soon get the message and relax into it.

> ## *Real Life Story*
> ### Elina – Friday Wrestle
>
> My husband has a 'wrestle' with our two boys on our bed every Friday night when he comes in from work. This has become a keenly awaited ritual in our family – a sign that the working week is finished and it's time to let our hair down and enjoy the weekend together as a family. The boys (and Dad) love it!

Time Outside

'Nature deficit disorder' is a growing concern. Make sure children's daily and weekly rhythms include time in the garden and green, outdoor places. Burn off toddler energy and experience the wonders of nature: double bonus! A child needs to play outside every day. A pre-bed night-time walk with a torch in the garden can be a special activity with Daddy or Mummy.

Cleaning Day Keeps the Cobwebs Away

I clean on a Saturday and now that my children are older we all help to make the house clean together (most of the time...). By creating a weekly rhythm for cleaning, it gets done on a regular basis, and my children learn life skills too. When children are encouraged to play 'cleaning chores' alongside you when young, cleaning together becomes a more natural activity, a team activity, a tribal custom!

A Soulful and Fun Rhythm for Parents

A weekly outing day does not have to be to a 'child' place that is primarily entertaining for children, such as the zoo or a mini-train park. You can also choose places that inspire parents: a botanical garden, a beach, an art gallery, a favourite café. With a little creativity, fun can be had by everyone. To help children enjoy more adult places, I recommend taking a child's backpack with food and small play items, or bringing dolly or a push-along bike.

Build activites that you personally enjoy into your weekly rhythm, to keep you feeling nourished and energised. Set aside time for swimming or yoga, a bath with aromatherapy oil, an afternoon walk in nature, reading, or a special craft project for those half hours while your children quietly play or sleep.

If you have family nearby, would your child enjoy an afternoon each week with them, while you have time to yourself or with your partner as a couple? A once-a-week date with yourself is a healthy rhythm for maintaining your wellbeing. If you do not have family, maybe you can connect with a friend who has children (children who your child is familiar with and happy to play with)? Perhaps you and your friend can have a regular arrangement to take turns minding each other's children, so you can each have some time to yourself every week or so.

Rhythm, Not Rigidity

It is fine if you don't feel like a walk on Walk Day, or if your children have their afternoon sleep in the pram or car rather than their beds or their special daytime sleep spot once in a while. Go with the flow and follow your intuition and your child's needs in the moment – and adapt to the weather conditions! This is a wonderful way to live; have a plan and a contingency plan.

Everybody's daily and weekly rhythms are unique. What feels right for you and your child? If you recognise that you are really busy, can you be conscious about it? Is it working?

Rhythms need to change and adapt to suit different children and different stages in their life. Keep observing your children: what do they need in a rhythm now?

If, in your household, children are with relatives or at childcare while parents work during the week, this doesn't mean there isn't a family rhythm. A lovely morning greeting and evening and bedtime routines help you all to connect at the start and end of the day. The early evenings could also include short activities in a simple weekly rhythm of days for baking, craft or massage. And you can have special meals at the weekend. (Sunday pancakes: yum!)

It is the ordinary moments of every day or week that form the memories of childhood, and get passed on to the next generation.

It is parents who must create the positive rhythms that will build a sense of stability, trust and joy in their children.

Once when I was teaching a class of seven year olds, we had been reading a book about whales. During question and comment time, a child piped up, 'Did you know that young whales really need their parents' attention? If they don't get attention, they will lie on their parent's blow hole so the parent can't breathe!' Wow, what a story!

I reflect that our own children stop us – in other ways! – because they, like young whales, need connection and attention. With a steady weekly rhythm, we can ensure that the attention they need is built in. They do not have to stop us and demand it.

Something to Try

Imagine that you are your child. Sit quietly and shut your eyes. Go through your child's day, or a part of it, in your mind's eye. Imagine the morning greeting, mealtimes, daily activities, rest time and the bedtime routine. How do they feel for your child? Are there changes you might make with your new awareness?

Happy Hurrying

If you are in a hurry to get out of the door in the mornings, being organised the night before can start a new day the right way up! Choose clothes and place them ready on a bedroom chair. Lay the breakfast table with bowls, cutlery and cereal boxes the night before. Your child could help before bed – playing waiter! How do you feel when staying at a bed and breakfast and the table is laid when you come downstairs? Pack bags and get lunchboxes and drink bottles ready in the evening too. This will help to reduce the morning stress, and allow for morning greetings and breakfast.

Play a fun game of 'beat the timer' together as you get dressed. 'Can we be dressed in five minutes? I bet we can't!' If you need to hurry out of the door, pretend that you are moving like cheetahs and not like snails, or flying like a rocket to the car.

Monthly Meetings

When my children were nine and eleven, we began having family meetings each month. The Chair, who took notes, also chose the treat for the meeting (a bar of chocolate – yum!). We began by celebrating an achievement that month for each person in the family (however simple), and followed with one grumble (only one!) to work on. 'Dad, can you please put your used teabag in the compost bin, and not leave it on the side of the sink?' These requests were noted so we could check the next month whether they had led to change. To end, we decided the family outing for the month: perhaps ten-pin bowling? Our children loved these meetings; they were a time to connect and build a tribe – even with the little grumble in the middle!

Real Life Story
Janoel – Home Days

I came to Lou's conscious parenting classes when my son, Khelan, was three. The very first session we had was on the importance of rhythm: a topic I don't think I had ever really considered. One of the first questions Lou asked us was whether we regularly spent a whole day at home. I sat back and thought: we had swimming day, playgroup day, Kindergarten days, library day and so on, but not one day of the week was dedicated to having a day at home. I committed to a home day in that instant, I think.

From then on, we had a day at home every week. Every single member of our family stays in the house or garden – apart from the occasional walk or bike ride. We all do different things. I love cooking and baking, my partner loves building things, we all enjoy the garden, and the kids just love being involved in anything we're doing! Often they'll puddle along beside us in our housework. At other times we'll organise things, like painting, drawing, reading stories or craft work (my son's ball of finger knitting is as big as my head – although rounder!) During the course of that first year of home days, we gave Khelan his own little garden, and it was such a pleasure for him to plant seeds and to watch them grow.

A whole day at home, with no 'Hurry, hurry, come on, let's get into the car' was – and is – a blessing. It switches my mindset so that I think about what I'm doing now – not just trying to get something finished in time to make it to the next activity. Now that Khelan's at school, it is more difficult to have a weekly home day, but we still create them whenever we can. Sometimes we have to say no to another social engagement, just so that we can slow down and take time out to be creative and nourish ourselves, our home and the environment. And be present for our children.

In Khelan's second year of school, along with a group of other parents, we decided to set up a Slow Day. We planned a few hours of talks, workshops and activities to inspire visitors to have their own regular Slow Day at home. The response from everyone we talked to was – and is – heartwarming: young and old nodded their heads and said, 'Yes! That's what we need!' We had fabulous support from our local traders, local council and the Community Environment Park where the Slow Day was held. Our story was covered in four local papers as well as a major daily newspaper and national radio: people liked the idea. Over six hundred people came along to enjoy the day, and the feeling from them was positive and grateful.

I invite you to commit to your own Slow Day at home – it will enrich you and your family, and make your home and our world a better place!

Checklist – Rhythms

1. Morning greetings, how does your child's day start – with warmth like the Sun?

2. Sit down together for breakfast and invite the three bears. (A little jug to pour the milk is a winner!)

3. If you'll be in a hurry, get organised with clothes, breakfast items and bags the night before.

4. To steer clear of meltdowns caused by hunger or tiredness, make sure children eat and rest regularly.

5. Invite children to help lay the table, cook the meal and pick some flowers for a vase.

6. Create a fun food rhythm and make a chopped fruit and vegetable plate into a plane, face or train!

7. At family mealtimes, connect with chat about daily news (parents are the role models for this).

8. Buy a candle and snuffer to add magic to meal times.

9. Say a blessing or give thanks before eating (where did the food come from?), to teach gratitude and awareness.

10. Is there time for imaginative play at home today?

11. Can we spend regular time outdoors: it's important for the toddler years – and all years after!

12. Avoid hurried life. Time is a precious gift for children.

13. Remember to keep breathing-in and breathing-out activities in balance during the day.

14. Ensure children have a nurturing rest or sleep in the afternoon.

15. Throw the bed sheet over the kitchen table, rest together and read stories.

16. Make teeth cleaning fun. What did each tooth do today?

17. Sing, stroke and love at bedtime for sweet dreams.

18. Try to make sure your child is getting 11–12 hours sleep at night, and is waking independently.

19. Create a weekly rhythm. Include activities your child enjoys (Baking Day, Bath Day, Park Day, Pancake Day).

20. When children are young, aim to have one or two days at home each week if possible – or more.

21. Allow treats and TV (if your children watch TV) in a predictable rhythm. This helps to avoid and limit tantrums.

Chapter Two
Yearly Fabulous Festivals

*The festivals are nodal points of the year that unite
us with the Spirit of the Universe.*

RUDOLF STEINER

Celebrating Family Festivals

Annual festivals like birthdays, Christmas and Easter, or your
own faith's celebrations, can become a source of happiness and
security in the life of a child, and of the whole family. Celebrations
create feelings of awe and magic, and the understanding that
life is sacred. Yearly family rhythms bring the three 'C's into
our homes: communication, creativity and connection. Festivals
warm the hearts of children and all those around them, creating
strong family bonds.

The festival customs that we celebrate have been passed down
for centuries. Have they lost their transformative inner power
in modern commercialised society? In *Festivals, Family and Food*
(Hawthorn Press), Diana Carey and Judy Large comment:

> Some feel that major holidays are also in a commercial
> domain, with Christmas decorations in the shops so
> rapidly followed by Easter ones that the themes become
> superficial and any meaning lost.

Introducing Rudolf Steiner's *The Festivals and their Meaning*
(Rudolf Steiner Press), Ann Druitt agrees:

What do the festivals mean to us today? There must be many people who carry around a question like this along with the bags of Christmas shopping, or find it knocking on some back door of the mind as they pass the annual offerings of chocolate eggs piled high on the supermarket shelves. Perhaps we must accept that the time-honoured rituals of the year have lost their once-vigorous social energy and are now declining into habit. Our ancient customs seem to have generated only customers.

This chapter gives simple and inspiring ideas to create joy, connection and family warmth during birthdays, Christmas and other festivals, aiming to honour the spirit of the occasion. To feed children's soul life – and ours too! – enjoy the simple magic and rhythm of these special days and events.

These major festivals are important, but remember that celebration takes place on a daily basis, too. Every daily blessing at the meal table is a thanksgiving. The seasons also hold a soul quality – a magic to be felt and experienced, not necessarily intellectually understood – and we will discuss them further in the next chapter.

Celebrating Children's Birthdays

Birthdays can enrich, inspire and honour a child's life, not just be about receiving presents. (Although presents, of course, are fun!) A birthday celebrates a unique life. Remember to hold a birthday celebration for everyone in your family, not just children. Please put on that crown, Dad!

Birthday Verse

The night before your child's birthday, as a loving ritual, you can say this Birthday Verse when you are tucking them in to bed, adding in the appropriate ages for your child:

When I have said my evening prayer,
And my clothes are folded on the chair,

And [Mummy/Daddy] switches off the light,
I'll still be [age] years old tonight.
But from the very break of day,
Before the children rise and play,
Before the greenness turns to gold,
Tomorrow I'll be [birthday age] years old!
[birthday number] candles on my cake;
[birthday number] kisses when I wake.

I have written this lovely verse on a card, kept in my special birthday basket, which I use to set up the birthday festivals each year.

The Birthday Story

Tell your child the magical Birthday Story, if this inspires you. I have heard this story in many formats and joined all the parts I like together. Here is my adapted version:

Once upon a time there lived a little soul. She lived above the stars, and her friends were the Moon, the stars and the Sun. One day the little soul was dancing and playing above the stars, which suddenly parted, and the little soul looked down, at a new and beautiful land. The little soul ran to her guardian angel and said, 'Today I saw a new and beautiful land. May I visit there please?'

The guardian angel replied, 'First you need to wait for three special gifts.' It wasn't long before the little soul received her three gifts. The Sun gave her a warm heart, the stars a bright light to shine all around herself, and the Moon a silver ribbon so that she would always be able to find her way back.

The little soul ran to her guardian angel once again, and said, 'I have received my three special gifts, now may I visit the new and beautiful land?'

Her guardian angel replied, 'Be patient, my child, it is almost your time.'

That night the little soul went to bed, and while she was asleep, she had the most beautiful dream. In the dream she visited the new land, where she saw many faces. She ran up to two special people, gave them a hug, and said 'Will you be my Mummy, and will you be my Daddy?'

And they said, 'Yes, we will!'

The next morning the little soul awoke, ran to her guardian angel once more and told him of her wonderful dream. The guardian angel said, 'It is now your time.'

The little soul was led to the rainbow bridge, where her guardian angel stopped her. 'There is one more thing I have to ask of you: your wings, please. You do not need them in this new and beautiful land. I will keep them safe for you, until your return.' The little soul took off her wings, and then her guardian angel led her by the hand across the rainbow bridge and into the arms of her new parents.

It has been [birthday age] years now since the little soul came to earth. When she arrived the first thing her mum and dad gave her was her name. They called her [your child's name]. There are many people in this new land who love her: her mummy and daddy, grandpa and grandma, and all her playgroup friends. The stars visit her every night, the Sun keeps her warm every day and sometimes the rainbow pays a visit.

And her guardian angel is always watching over her.

You may have to practice this story a few times, to say it without crying! It reminds us of the preciousness of life and families, of how we chose our parents, and the uniqueness of every child on the earth. It whispers of the wonders and comforts of the spiritual world.

The Birthday Story can be told as a bedtime tale during the week leading up to, or the night before, a birthday. It can be told as a puppet play (using little dolls and play cloths) on the actual day, at the party, or just for your family's pleasure. This story enriches the lives of children: I think of it as a 'treasure tale'.

The Birthday Table

On the eve of a birthday (once you have read the verse!), when your child is in bed, it is lovely to set up a special birthday table. Children love this in the morning. Put a beautifully coloured play cloth on the table, and make a birthday spiral (a circle or spiral of candles –

perhaps tea-lights in glass jars – the same number of candles as your child's new age), include photos of your child with his loved ones, at various ages. Around the table add special crystals, precious things from nature and one large candle from which to light the smaller ones. Now you are set for tomorrow's birthday ceremony!

A Suggestion

Buy a basket from a secondhand shop to hold the birthday celebration cloths, candles, crown, verse and story. This makes it easier to set up the birthday festival for each family member. The festival grows in love and joy over the years. Your children look forward to being honoured for who they are – their birthdays enrich their soul life.

A Birthday Ceremony

Make a crown out of gold card or felt, or buy a birthday crown and cloak. Your child, adorned with her crown and cloak, lights each candle from the big candle (or, if she is too young, you light the candles). When one candle is lit, each family member tells a little story about the child in her first year, for example, remembering her favourite toy – any funny and loving memories. On to the next candle, which represents the second year in her life. Tell a loving tale from the child's life from one to two years, and so on, until all the candles have been lit and stories told. After the stories, each family member can give the child a special wish.

The unique child has been loved. The journey of a sacred soul to the earth has been honoured. The spiritual foundation has been laid. Now it is time to open the presents! In our house, the birthday person chooses where to go for a special tea: a night to remember.

Parents can set the birthday table up for each other (with the help of their children). Take time to share and celebrate every family member's birthday. Children love to hear tales about their parents. Tell parents' stories in ten-year increments: 'From birth to ten, Daddy had a dog named Poppy. Poppy was cheeky and ate some of Daddy's clothes!'

Birthday girl

A Time of Reflection

As a mother or father, spend some time in reflection on your child's birthing day. Remember the birth, and think about the loving connection you two have together (well, most of the time!). Recognise that, on a deep level, your two souls choose to be together. Although you may not always see it, you are perfect for each other! It's worth finding time for reflection on your own birthday, too. Perhaps take yourself off somewhere alone, surrounded by nature, to contemplate who you are as a unique person and what you individually bring to your family and the world. Feel your unique essence in this lifetime and celebrate it.

Loving words

Each year my favourite part of my birthday is the words in my husband's card. We fill both sides of the card with writing, a great time to express!

Now my son is fourteen, and he no longer looks for hugs, hand-holding or laps to sit on, he does receive a card with our many loving thoughts? Yes, the tradition carries on, and Jayson feels the power of love and words on his birthday.

Birthday Present Hunt!

My children love the game of 'Present Hunt with Clues'. (And so did I!) This birthday game can be played even before your child can read: you read the clues for your child, who hunts down the presents. For example, a clue, such as 'I love to clean clothes!' is left on the bedside table. At the washing machine the next clue is discovered and so on, until, after five clues or so, the presents are found. As children grow older, the clues can get more difficult. Last year, my son asked to write the clues for his eleven-year-old sister: the family tradition is being passed on!

Birthday Parties

With today's fast-paced life and commercialised entertainment, it is lovely to have a traditional birthday party. A party at home is a connecting and special time (and it saves money!). A traditional party is full of simple, inspiring pleasures for children. Here are a few pointers to guide you on your way.

A party in our house is a major festival, with the build-up and planning being just as much fun as the party itself. Involve the children in making the invitations, planning the menu, making paper chains, wrapping the Pass the Parcel, cooking the pizza on the day, making the birthday cake, creating little items for the goody bags and selecting the games. As with Christmas, the build-up to a party can be just as exciting as the day itself, so take four weeks to prepare. Of course, this preparation time consists of much communication, connection and creativity.

Invitations

Be creative and make your own invitations: now is the time to bring out the quality crayon blocks mentioned in this book's craft chapter. Use them to shade rainbows, or use paint to make handprints!

Time Length

One-and-a-half hours in the morning is usually plenty of time for small children. Any longer and all involved get frazzled! Once they are older, the party length can be extended.

Goody Bags

Make goody bags from brown paper bags, which can be drawn on by your child. Have fun decorating calico bags with fabric paints or, if you're feeling adventurous, tie dye. Think of a little craft project to make as party gifts (look through a simple craft book). Include bubbles, crystals, a packet of seeds, packets of natural sweets or small plain chocolate bars.

How Many Children?

I have heard that the rule of thumb is to invite the same number of children as your child's age. This is not always possible – a few more are sometimes needed for party games – but big is often not better, indeed it can be very overwhelming for a little one – and for parents too!

Arrival and the Present Game

Place a circle of cushions on the floor, awaiting little bottoms. Set up a table for presents. A vase of flowers on a coloured cloth will make this table look special. When the guests arrive, the children sit on the cushions and the birthday child sits in the middle, blindfolded. Each child in turn gives their present and says, 'Happy Birthday [birthday child's name]' The birthday child guesses whose voice it is and, while everyone watches, opens the present.

This starts the party off in a calm, fun way. Some children may not want to join in. This is fine, and adults can do it for them. Young children require a model to imitate, so maybe practise the game before the party, with you in the middle, so young children can see how it's played.

An alternative game for receiving the presents is the Matching Card Game. Draw two identical sets of cards showing flowers, boats, cars, suns, rainbows or other simple pictures. Your child can help you to choose, draw or colour the pictures, depending on their age.

Leave one card on top of each cushion, and give the birthday child a basket with the other matching set, and sit them in the middle. The birthday child chooses one of their cards and calls out what's in the picture. The child with the matching card then gives their present to the birthday child. Children love this simple game.

It is wonderful to make the present-giving ceremony a fun and honouring time. Otherwise the paper will be ripped off and discarded in a frenzy of excitement. Either of the games I've suggested starts the party in a respectful and loving way.

Most children are interested in what's behind a present wrapper! Who isn't?

Party Games

With the children already in a circle at the end of the present-giving ceremony, play simple party games. I tend to play the same number of games as the age of the child. Try to avoid competitive ones, especially those which have only one winner. Party games for all ages can be found in the superb book by Anne and Peter Thomas, *The Children's Party Book: For birthdays and other occasions* (Floris Books).

The party games I have played with young children to five years include:

Pass the Parcel: under each wrapper hide the same little treat. Young children love to pass and unwrap, and this keeps out the element of competition. I place a number of wishing stones, crystals or knick-knacks in the middle (or blow-bubble wands or chocolate bars!), for everyone to share.

Children love to sing! In the middle of the circle, place cards with favourite song titles on them. Choose a child to pick a card, which tells everyone what to sing. Popular classics include: 'Here We Go Round the Mulberry Bush', 'Incy Wincy Spider', 'The Wheels on the Bus' and 'Ring A Rosie'.

As your children grow, new games can be added to this circle time:

'Guess Who is Hiding Under the Blanket?' is a fun game, if the children know each other. One child leaves the room, and another child is chosen to hide under a blanket in the middle of the circle. The child out of the room returns. 'Who is now missing?'

'Changes' is also a fun game. A child is chosen to leave the room and change something about her appearance: roll a sock down, take a hair slide out, or unbutton one hole in a top. The children then guess what has changed about her appearance

After a few party games, it is time to eat!

Food and Drink

Party food can be nutritious and fun: homemade pizzas, fruit kebabs, homemade popcorn and mini pancakes, corn chips and vegetable sticks with dips, natural potato chips. Fruit juice with sparkling mineral water is a party treat! Refrain from putting lollies and sweet foods on the table or all the more substantial food will be left behind and a sugar fix will reign! After the savoury food and fruit has been eaten, as a finale, cut and eat the cake.

A homemade birthday cake is fun. Decorate a simple sponge cake. For girls, 'beetroot juice' icing is great. Mix the icing with a little of the juice from a can of beetroot. It will go bright pink, with no artificial colouring! Otherwise, decorate with fresh flowers. For boys make the birthday cake into the number for their age and keep it plain or cover it in chocolate or white icing. It is easy to have parties free from food colouring and chemicals. It is the candles and the 'blowing out' that children love, and, of course, the singing of 'Happy Birthday to You'!

After the food, a little playtime to run and be free hits the mark. Perhaps offer face painting or craft outside, or hold a treasure hunt for the goody bags. 'Giant's Footsteps' or 'What's the Time, Mr Wolf?' are fun outdoor games to play.

A Good Ending!

Have a clear ending – a thank you and a goodbye with a goody bag – and then the party does not drag on too long. When adults are chatting and tired children are playing, accidents, quarrels and upsets happen, and the energy is lost. Hold the party in a structured, fun way, and say goodbye! Everyone leaves feeling inspired and happy, and not too tired. You can use the telling of the Birthday Story as a nice quiet end.

Themed Parties

A little fancy dress is fun! My husband and I always try to be the entertainment. We have put on a circus, held the guinea pigs and rabbits, and face painted. Our themes have included rabbits, fairies, fishing, planes and the circus! Children do not expect you to be professional entertainers, they just want to have a simple, good time. At a young age they love to see their parents participate. (Teenagers may cringe!) Put on a magician's cloak or be a storyteller, young children are easy to please (this is part of their charm).

Sustainable Birthdays and Parties

Each step of the way, be conscious of the earth. Can you use recycled paper for your invitations? Brown paper or fabric for the goody bags? Recyclable or reusable cups and plates for the food? Fabric (even charity shop pillow cases!) can be used to wrap the presents. Cloth flags can decorate the room and homemade food has less packaging. Have fun making your birthdays sustainable: a gentle footprint on the earth leads to an inspired way of living.

Give it a go!

Be courageous! Hold a party, especially when your children are young. It saves you a fortune! Keep to a small number of children, a short time, and a structure of fun, non-competitive games. The planning, as well as the party, becomes a creative and connecting experience for the whole family.

Your child's birthday is complete for another year. Woven through the birthday has been magic, joy and love, a time to remember, and something to look forward to, next year...

A Word from a Dad – Michael

It was my mother's birthday last week. She always fudged answers about her age, so she may have been five years older than we realised. I wish I had celebrated my parents' birthdays when we were younger. I like the idea of a birthday table (and celebration and stories) for the adults in a family too. The message children get to express is, 'I'm glad you are here, Mum and Dad!'

A Word from Seven-year-old Jayson

Birthday parties at home are fun. I like to prepare for the party. My favourite thing is helping Mum to cook the cake and snacks. I set up the birthday table for my sister.

Real Life Story
Ronia – A Recycled Birthday

We received an invitation for a birthday party for one of my child's friends. This invitation was quite different to the usual party invitations we received. This was to be a birthday that would make a difference to the environment. The invitation stated, 'pre-loved or recycled presents only'. What a fascinating idea! All I would have to do is walk into the toy room or secondhand shop, collect a few toys and wrap them up – in recycled paper, of course! I explained to my three-year-old that he could choose a toy to give away for a 'long, long time!'

I likened the experience to sharing, or taking turns, because we have so many toys. I talked to him about the Earth: how there are millions of toys being thrown out each year around the world, including plastic ones that will stay underground as rubbish for much longer than our lives. It worked: over the course of an hour, great internal learning took place. The end result was he donated a red fire truck to be a present (he had two such toys).

At the party, I noticed immediately the handmade wrapping paper, tied with wool, the stickers, stamps and finger paint galore, and the unique homemade birthday cards that were for one special three-year-old boy. As he unwrapped the gifts, he did not care they were 'pre-loved'. They were his, now, and they were new to him! That is where the glory was.

I will always remember this special recycled birthday party and I hope you do too.

Real Life Story
Vicki – A Montessori Birthday

Here is the Montessori way of celebrating a birthday: lay down a piece of fabric and place labels telling the months of the year around the fabric (this is optional), along with pictures of the seasons (also optional). In the middle of the circle is a candle representing the Sun. The birthday child stands up, holding a globe of the Earth, at the month he or she was born, and proceeds to walk around the candle (the Sun). While the child is walking around, sing, 'The Earth goes around the Sun, [child's name], the Earth goes around the Sun, and every time it goes around, another year is done.'

The child walks around as many times as he or she has lived on the Earth. Often a list of memories will be recalled for each year of the child's life.

Celebrating Christmas

The spirit of Christmas has been lost amongst the presents! Christmas has the potential to be so much more than a commercial extravaganza.

Christmas is a sacred time for those with a Christian belief. It can also be a sacred time for those of other faiths, uncertain faith, or no faith at all. It is an important part of the world calendar and provides a yearly family rhythm; time to share, time to give.

The Christmas celebration does not need to be bound to a specific or excluding religious philosophy: the story of the birth of Jesus is an archetypal spiritual account of goodness and truth. You can share it with young children in a simple and beautiful way. We do not have to be of any particular religion, or a church attendee, to celebrate the birth of the special child who turned into a man with an exceptionally loving heart, and who shared kindness, healing and compassion with all on Earth. On our journey as human beings, these are qualities that are well worth aspiring to!

The birth of Jesus is worth sharing and celebrating, as are the great spiritual stories from many different faiths. I did not tell my young children the whole Jesus story, his life and ending crucifixion, as I felt this was too adult. Children are touched by the wonderful tale of a special child, carried while in the womb by a humble donkey, born in a stable, with animals looking on, and being visited by shepherds and kings alike!

Christmas Carols

Singing Christmas carols together as a family is uplifting and connecting. Carols are steeped in history. Do you remember your childhood favourites? Buy a simple Christmas carol book, like Miriam Farbey's *The First Noel* (Dorling Kindersley), and sing around the tree together at night. If you are lucky enough to have people who play instruments at your house, a piano or guitar accompaniment sets the scene. Don't think you can't sing – children do not notice! It is your heartfelt intention, not your singing voice, which is important.

Advent Calendars

It is best to steer clear, where possible, from Advent calendars that create a lust for chocolate (and very cheap chocolate at that!). Chocolate in the morning is not the healthiest way to start the day! We already have one festival of the year dedicated to chocolate (you know, the bunny one). Do we want to dedicate all celebrations to the almighty dark, smooth stuff? It's stimulating to the taste buds, but there are many other ways to enrich the soul!

Purchase a beautiful Advent calendar that can be used each year, or make one for your child. A fabric or wooden one can hold little gifts, and messages of love. A fun family ritual is to tie a line of string across the room, and on it hang 24 numbered brown paper bags in a row. Imagine the excitement of opening a bag each day. A little gift, homemade treat, note or picture is inside.

Advent Spiral

A wooden Advent spiral contains 24 candles and holders. One extra candle is lit every day of December, until 24 are being lit on Christmas Eve – quite a sight! A little candle-lighting ceremony can take place with a Christmas carol or story each night. This provides a lovely ritual at home for Christmas time.

The Advent Table

To set up a magical Advent table in your home, think about Christmas in November! Once an Advent table is set up one year, it's easy to re-create the following year. Clear away your seasonal table (we discuss seasonal tables in detail in the next chapter) or use a plain low table. The two coloured cloths you require are red (on the table) and blue (as the hanging backdrop). These are the two colours that Mary is usually shown wearing in depictions of the nativity. The blue represents the spirit world coming down to meet us, and the red is for love. Place four special Advent candles (large candles in holders) on the table.

Now is the time to honour all the kingdoms on the Earth. On the first Sunday of Advent (count back four Sundays from Christmas Day), light one candle and introduce the mineral kingdom to the table. Collect and display special crystals, stones and rocks found by the children around their home and garden. Think of how minerals serve us, including the ones in our mouth and body: teeth and bones!

The second Sunday, the first and second candles are lit, adding the plant kingdom. A vase of flowers, berries or holly picked by children, or a pot plant can be placed on the table. As an adult, show reverence by contemplating and giving thanks to the different elements that make up our planet. The plant kingdom adds beauty, nourishment and the whisperings of spirit to the Earth.

On the third Sunday, light three candles; it is time for the animals to come! The stable can appear – with animals in and around it – waiting for Mary, Joseph and Jesus. The stable can be bought, or made from a cardboard box; it is the love and intent that is important, not what you spend. Again, contemplate the animal kingdom that shares the Earth alongside us.

On the fourth Sunday, all four candles are now alight, and Mary and Joseph appear. Buy a nativity set, or make felt dolls and animals, or look for a set in a secondhand shop. Maybe there is already a nativity scene in your extended family? Ask around.

Mary can slowly arrive: she can magically start from the other side of the room on her journey to the stable. Each night of the week, Mary, Joseph and the donkey, aided by invisible helpers, mysteriously move closer. On Christmas Eve, they arrive at the stable. The little manger awaits baby Jesus. When younger, my children ran to the table on Christmas morning shouting, 'Baby Jesus is here!' After a month of anticipation, a magical moment has arrived.

A star appears over the stable on Christmas night and the table continues after Christmas Day. On Boxing Day, there is a visit from the shepherds with their sheep! On January 6, the time has come for the kings. The kings can also travel from afar, across the room, as Mary and Joseph did. The table is now complete. The story of the birth of Jesus has been magically woven into the Advent table.

A Countdown in Stars

Another Advent calendar idea is to use the blue cloth that is the backdrop of the Advent table. On each December morning, your child can place a gold sticky star (the type some teachers use) on the blue cloth. This is simple but stunning, and satisfying for the child. What an amazing sight on Christmas day: 24 stars shining over the Advent table!

Story Telling

Stories provide enriching moments during the lead-up to Christmas day. Good books include Georg Dreizig's *The Light in the Lantern* (Wynstones Press) and Estelle Bryer and Janni Nicol's *Christmas Stories Together* (Hawthorn Press). These are simple chapter books for older children (age five onwards). They contain a story for each day of Advent, representing each of the four elements: the mineral, plant, animal and human kingdoms. After the child places a star on the blue backdrop, opens a pocket or window on their calendar, or lights a candle in the spiral for each day of Advent, read a story.

Storybooks that describe the journey of Mary and Joseph to Bethlehem, the birth of Jesus and his special visitors add to the wonder of the Advent table. Remember to keep the story of Jesus simple. Bring the same books out each year at this time, and build a magical Christmas rhythm.

In our home, we regard Jesus (along with Buddha, Muhammad, Krishna and others), as a living example of enlightenment. Celebrate the Christmas story because of the simple goodness and inspiration it holds. It enriches our hearts.

Father Christmas

Father Christmas originates from the legend of Saint Nicholas, a person who loved and was kind to all children. Steer clear of that Father Christmas who is used as an instrument of control: 'Father Christmas only visits good children.' He loves all children! Childhood is a magical and sacred time, requiring respect and celebration.

At our house, we sprinkle oats on the lawn for the reindeers to eat and also sparkle-dust so the reindeers can see the way in the starlight. We leave out a carrot for them, and a glass of milk and a mince pie for Father Christmas. Christmas Eve is a special, unique time for children, and when they do find out he is probably not coming down the chimney – usually they ask around the age of nine – they can be told that the spirit of Saint Nicholas, his love for children, and the sacredness of childhood live on always.

The Christmas Tree

The Christmas tree is evergreen: it is vibrant all year round, and symbolises the ongoing nature of a loving heart and of spirit. You can bring these qualities to mind when looking at and decorating your family tree.

The tree can be decorated in a fun and creative way, and

children love to help. Sew popcorn together on a line of cotton thread (popcorn tinsel!) and make fabric stars, paper chains and clay hangings. Fairy lights, of course, add sparkle!

Christmas Craft

The gift of giving is sacred; start preparing and making Christmas presents and cards early or the rush may lead you to buy rather than make.

If children's own preparation of little gifts is filled with joy, warmth and love for the recipients, then those children feel enriched in themselves. That, says Brigette Barz in *Festivals with Children* (Floris Books), is the genuine preparation for Christmas.

Christmas Cards

Design your own cards by cutting out a Christmas tree or star shape from a young child's painting (use a cookie cutter as a stencil). Mount this painted shape onto coloured card, and stick gold stars on too, with a special wish.

Gingerbread Recipe

With this gingerbread recipe and star-shaped or Christmas tree-shaped cookie cutters, children can make wonderful gifts. People love to receive a homemade gift from a child.

* 125 g (4½ oz) butter (at room temperature)
* 100 g (3½ oz) of brown sugar
* 120 ml (4 fl oz) of golden syrup
* 1 egg (separated)
* 375 g (13 oz) plain flour
* 1 tbs ground ginger
* 1 tsp mixed spice
* 1 tsp bicarbonate of soda
* icing sugar to decorate

Preheat oven to 180° C (350° F), and brush two baking trays with melted butter to grease lightly.

Use an electric mixer to beat the butter and sugar in a bowl until pale and creamy. Add the golden syrup and egg yolk and beat until combined. Stir in the flour, ginger, mixed spice and bicarbonate of soda. Turn onto a lightly floured surface and knead until smooth. Press dough into a ball. Cover with plastic wrap and place in the fridge for 30 minutes to rest.

You can use this time to make the icing. Place the egg white in a clean, dry bowl. Use a (washed and dried) electric mixer to beat until soft peaks form. Gradually add the icing sugar and beat until stiff peaks form. Cover with a plate and place in the fridge.

Returning to the biscuits, place the dough between two sheets of baking paper and roll it out until it is about 4 mm (⅙ in) thick. Use Christmas star or tree cutters to create biscuits. Place the biscuits on trays leaving space between them as they will expand while cooking. Repeat with any excess dough.

Bake the biscuits for 10 minutes or until brown. Remove from the oven and transfer to a rack to cool.

The biscuits can be decorated, and bagged or wrapped as gifts.

Or you can create a Christmas tree using different sized star-shaped biscuits. Place the prepared icing in a small piping bag (alternatively, use a little plastic bag with a small hole cut in the corner). Assemble a wonderful tree by placing a large star on the bottom. Put a little icing in the middle to stick a smaller star on top, turning the points to face different directions. Continue to build, using icing to stick, placing small- or medium-sized stars alternately with large stars, and layering up.

What a sight! Children love to assemble this gingerbread tree every Christmas. Make small trees, using tiny and medium biscuits, to give as gifts, or a large biscuit tree for the family to share.

More craft ideas using Christmas cookie cutters

You can use Christmas cookie cutters to cut clay stars and trees out of a fast-drying clay like Das. Put a hole in while the clay is soft, and decorate by pushing on beads before the shapes dry, or by painting them afterwards. Ribbon threaded through the hole turns your clay shape into a lovely hanging Christmas decoration.

You can also use cookie cutters as templates to draw on felt or on Christmas fabric. Sew two identical shapes together and stuff, then stitch a loop on the top for a soft homemade Christmas decoration!

Baking and crafts are lovely Christmas family activities. The gift of giving, from our own hands!

An Ethical and Recycled Christmas

We can buy gifts that benefit people in need rather than large corporations. Seek out catalogues of ethical and fair trade gifts. Make Christmas a recycled affair by reusing last year's Christmas cards for new present labels. Buy recycled Christmas wrap, make your own cards or purchase them from a charity outlet. When we go ethical shopping our purchase gives to others around the world: Happy Conscious Christmas!

Secondhand goods can make great Christmas presents for a child. Here is my funny version of a popular Christmas song:

The Twelve Days of Christmas
(or Twelve Trips to the secondhand Shop!)

One wooden dolls' house
Two sandpit saucepans
Three cotton bedspreads
Four little teapots
Five strings of beads
Six carved bowls
Seven shiny egg cups
Eight wicker baskets
Nine tiny toy cars
Ten nursery rhyme books
Eleven crocheted doilies
Twelve jazzy outfits
And a lovely (if you're lucky!) rocking horse!

Three Things List

Each Christmas and birthday, I consider my Three Things list when looking for presents:

1. A game or outside activity
2. A story (for reading fun)
3. A craft activity (to be creative together)

For younger children, include a movement game to play outdoors. Movement fires up children's brain neurons, it gives them exercise and it's fun. Examples of outdoor movement toys and games include: balls, swing ball, chalk for hopscotch, a kite, a pogo stick or a frisbee.

For older children (from seven onwards), a family board game is an excellent gift. Family games nights help build bonds, especially once children have reached an age when winning and losing are not such dramatic events. Families that play together, stay together!

Books are important and special, particularly in our fast-paced and electronic world. They encourage us to snuggle together, connect and imagine. The love of reading is fostered by providing inspiring books for children and reading together every day. Write a personal message to the child in the front cover, with the birthday or Christmas date.

Craft kits provide an activity to do together over the Christmas holidays. Kit ideas include: paper flowers, homemade soap, wooden cars and boats, paper aeroplanes and necklaces. Children's hands and hearts love to create; craft is a powerful and connecting activity, and it's fun!

On Christmas morning we hand out presents from under the tree to each person, and take it in turns to open one gift, thus avoiding a frenzied present opening time, and allowing time for appreciation (in the giving and the receiving).

Enjoy this Sacred Time

How we feel about Christmas time reflects in our children's experience. Are we busy, stressed and fed-up, or do we hold a feeling of happiness in our heart? Celebrate this festival together, and stoke the fire of Christmas joy. Watch the embers fly!

The spiritual world is close at Christmas time; it is an opportunity for deep reflection, contemplation, compassion and joy. Instead we may rush from shop to shop. Take the time to celebrate and build the sacredness of this festival throughout the month of December, together. Young children will then carry lifelong inspiring memories in their hearts, of giving, singing and creating at Christmas time. They soon forget which presents they received, but the family memories last forever!

Easter Ideas

We always left out a rabbit figure and carrot, which of course was seriously nibbled in the morning!

Hot Cross Bun Recipe

Here is a great hot cross bun recipe for Easter family baking. Children love to knead and watch the dough rise. Even though this takes time, it is a beautiful ritual on a home day during the Easter break.

* 300 ml (10½ fl oz) milk
* 2 eggs, lightly beaten
* 600 g (21 oz) plain flour
* 1½ tsp mixed spice
* pinch of salt
* 50 g (1 ¾ oz) caster sugar
* 40 g (1½ oz) butter
* 250 g (8 ¾ oz) of currants
* 2 x 7 g (¼ oz) packets dried yeast

Combine the flour, yeast, sugar, mixed spice, salt and currants in a large bowl.

Melt the butter in a small saucepan, add the milk and heat until lukewarm. Add the warm milk mixture and eggs to the current mixture.

Use a flat-bladed knife to mix it all into a dough, until it is almost coming together. Then use your hands to finally form the dough.

Turn the dough onto a floured surface and knead until smooth (10 minutes).

Place the dough into a lightly oiled bowl, cover with a clean tea towel and set it aside in a warm draft-free place for 1–1½ hours, or until the dough doubles in size.

Punch the dough down to its original size and knead it again on a floured surface. Divide it into twelve evenly-sized balls, place the balls on a greased tray, cover them with a cloth, and set them aside in warm place for 30 minutes, or until they double in size.

Preheat the oven to 190° C (375° F). Make crosses. For the crosses rub together 50 g (1¾ oz) of plain flour and 2 tbs of butter. Add water to make a soft pastry. Roll the pastry between your fingers to make a snake. Lay two lengths over each bun to make a cross.

Bake for 20–25 minutes or until cooked through. Eat warm with butter – yum!

Easter Egg Hunt

When setting up an Easter egg hunt with mini chocolate eggs, buy a packet of different colours and allocate a colour to each sibling. Or if you are using a single colour of mini eggs, collect them in baskets, and then at the end an adult can share them out. This makes the game equal and fun, without older siblings finding many more eggs on their longer legs!

Painted Hardboiled Eggs (family faces!)

When I was young, my dad's passion was model aeroplanes. He would use oil paint to create the aeroplane's markings. One Easter, he decided to surprise us in the morning by using this paint to decorate four hard-boiled eggs with our family members' faces. To our surprise we were met with these painted eggs on the breakfast table. What fun it was, each trying to find our own face – especially as Dad is not the greatest artist! This tradition continues each year, and now happens on my own children's Easter breakfast table. I reflect on my dad's special time of creativity, which cost no money and has been passed down the generations...

This year we dyed our hard-boiled eggs using bowls of boiling water, a tablespoon of vinegar and food colouring, natural dyes can be used too. Mix food colouring to create purple, orange and green as well as the primary colours. Place the egg on a spoon and coat it in the colouring for as long as it takes to turn the desired shade. Leave it to dry on paper. A bowl full of coloured eggs on the dining-room table looks stunning.

Egg-Cracking Competition

A friend taught me this game, passed down through the generations in her family. On Easter Friday morning, every family member holds a coloured hard-boiled egg in one hand. Tap your egg against someone else's egg. The first one to crack is out, and eats their egg. Which is the winning egg in the family?

This is a fun game to play with older children, when winning and losing is not a tearful but a laughing event!

Easter String Game

At a recent parenting workshop, one lady shared her Easter family game. Her mother tied a different colour piece of wool for each child from a starting point and made a trail of wool around the house. At the end were that child's eggs! Can you imagine this Easter game through a child's eyes – how much fun! I wish I had played it when my children were young – we could even have taken the wool to the garden and back! Have a go and let me know...

> *Something to Think About*
>
> What do you remember from your own childhood
> birthdays and Christmas times or special family festivals?
> How can you enrich these yearly occasions for your child?

Two Stories of Multi-Cultural Festivals

Dana – My Jewish Upbringing

The festival I enjoyed as a child was Passover (the Hebrew term
is *Pesach*). The whole idea of Passover is to tell the story of the
Exodus, when the Israelites were freed from slavery in Egypt.

A special part of Passover is the Seder, a special meal that is
held on the first night of Passover. During the Seder, the story
of the Exodus from Egypt is retold, and children are encouraged
to get involved by joining in, singing the songs and answering
questions. The Seder is critical to Passover because it is about
teaching the children their past and ensuring that this important
history is passed on from generation to generation.

During the Seder, there are five fun events that stand out for
a child.

The youngest child of the family sings the *Ma Nishtana*
(translation: 'what makes tonight different from all other nights').
It is a song based on questions that encourage discussion about the
significance of certain symbolic things that are done throughout
the meal.

The hiding of the Afikoman 'dessert' encourages excitement
among children. During the Seder, the leader breaks the middle
piece of Matzah (unleavened bread) into two, and sets aside
the larger portion as the Afikoman. The Afikoman is hidden
somewhere in the house for the children to find, and a prize
is offered for finding it. As a child, this was the game I most
looked forward to! Even though the Seder is long, the Afikoman
managed to keep me awake and alert. And the prize for finding
the Afikoman was always very rewarding!

We sang and recited the ten plagues of Egypt, and then traditionally dipped fingers into a glass of red wine for each and every plague. I always loved the singing and participating in the ritual.

Other songs, such as 'Echad Mi Yodea' (translation: 'who knows one'), are fun tunes, with lots of actions and repetition.

Finally, there is the Passover Seder plate: arranged on a plate are six symbolic items that have special significance in the retelling of the story of the Exodus from Egypt. Often these foods are only eaten on Passover, so they are something to look forward to. My favourite was always the Charoset, which is a sweet mixture of apples and walnuts, and the hardboiled egg, which we eat with salt water, representing the tears of difficult times, which have been overcome.

Nira – a Hindu Childhood

In the Hindu tradition, every month there is a festival to honour different gods or different aspects of life, for example, harvest festival. When reflecting on her own childhood, the festival my own mother looked forward to the most was Diwali, the festival of lights. During this festival, we depict knowledge overcoming ignorance or, to put it another way, light overcoming darkness. My mother looked forward to the firecrackers and everybody receiving a new set of clothes. Specific sweet meats and dishes are prepared. My own memories of Diwali are of being scared witless by the noise of crackers, but at night being delighted by the colourful fireworks.

Reflection

We are not aiming for a perfect day. Real parents create real lives, which include times of tears, sibling squabbles and tired parents, even on special days...

Checklist – Family Festivals

1. Share the Birthday Verse on the eve of your children's birthdays.

2. Tell the Birthday Story to your children.

3. Set up an honouring birthday table: candles, photos and special things!

4. Hold a birthday ceremony (including a crown) at the birthday table. Tell a story for each year, and make a wish.

5. Take time to reflect on your birthday and your children's birthdays.

6. Hold a simple birthday party; have fun preparing for the event together.

7. Bring the 'Christ' back into Christmas, if you are inspired.

8. Sing favourite Christmas carols together, especially if anyone in your family plays an instrument.

9. Set up an Advent table. Celebrate the four kingdoms on the Earth and Jesus' birth.

10. Celebrate the 24 days of December with an Advent spiral, or a backdrop of stars to an Advent table. Be creative!

11. Include inspiring simple Christmas stories in your Advent.

12. Decorate the evergreen tree.

13. Celebrate Father Christmas, keeping the true spirit of Saint Nicholas alive.

14. Help children to make their own cards and small gifts for loved ones.

15. Hold the energy of awe, excitement, reverence and family connections at Christmas time and your child will share these attitudes with you!

16. Make hot cross buns as a yearly Easter ritual, and play the egg hunting 'Easter-String' game.

17. If my dad can paint an egg, with his limited creative ability, so can you!

18. Create a yearly rhythm with your own faith's special days.

Chapter Three
Celebrating the Seasons

When we tug at a single thing in nature, we find it attached to
the rest of the world...

JOHN MUIR

The Gifts of Nature

Nature enhances our lives, reduces stress and creates balance and healing, sometimes without us even knowing it.

The journal *Science* reported a study of hospital patients that I find interesting: one group of patients had a room with a window view of a tree; the other group's view was a brick wall.

Records on patients' recovery after cholecystectomy in a suburban Pennsylvania hospital between 1972 and 1981 were examined to determine whether assignment to a room with a window view of a natural setting might have restorative influences. The surgical patients assigned to rooms with windows looking out on a natural scene had shorter post-operative hospital stays, received fewer negative evaluative comments in nurses' notes and took fewer potent analgesics than matched patients in similar rooms with windows facing a brick building wall (April 27, 1984, Vol 224, no. 4647, pp.420-421).

Similarly, research at the University of Illinois discussed in Sue Palmer's book *Toxic Childhood* (Orion) suggests that contact with nature can have a significant 'detoxing' effect on children with attention deficit disorders, and 'the greener the setting, the greater the relief'. In contrast, researchers found that indoor activities like watching television or outdoor activity in paved or non-green areas increased attention deficit.

Richard Louv, author of the wonderful book *Last Child in the Woods: Saving our Children from Nature Deficit Disorder* (2006), discusses the benefits of nature for children, and explains that children's symptoms of ADD and ADHD decrease when out in nature, as do the stress levels of both adults and children. On his website (www.richardlouv.com), he states:

> The future will belong to the nature-smart – those individuals, families, businesses and political leaders who develop a deeper understanding of the transformative power of the natural world, and who balance the virtual with the real. The more high tech we become, the more nature we need.

This chapter will share ideas on how to build a deeper connection with nature in family life.

Outdoor Adventures

Spend time outside every day, in the garden or local park. It is really important for children to have unstructured time outside, to dig to China or watch a bug (see Chapter 7 for outdoor play items to inspire children's outdoor adventures).

Visit places of natural beauty for family picnics. Is there a pond with ducks, a beach, woodland, botanical gardens or parkland area nearby? Create a weekly outing to get a nature fix! If you enjoy it, your child is more likely to enjoy it too. Point out natural wonders, picnic with a special rug and basket, encourage your children to pack and take a rucksack each, tell a story during a little walk, make walking sticks with branches and collect items for the seasonal table.

During the warmer months, simply eat your lunch or dinner outside, on a table or a blanket in the garden, under the shade of a tree. Nature holds the key to physical, emotional and spiritual enrichment and development in children.

Something to Try

On one of your regular walks, as well as noticing the seasonal changes in nature, take a plastic bag and pick up litter. This simple exercise teaches our children a respect for our earth.

Camping Fun

Camping is a wonderful activity for children; as part of a yearly rhythm, find a National Park or campground, maybe just for one night at first! Children need not go far, they like to put the tent up in the garden on a summer evening!

Camping is always an adventure. First we build our own house, like magic, with poles and cloth! Second, we sleep in bags like caterpillars. Third, we stay outside all the time and see many natural things: stars, birds, campfires, animals. It is easy to play with sticks and dirt and feel the grass beneath our feet. Fourth, we slow down, feel the breeze, sometimes rain, and touch the Earth.

Seasonal Rhythms

The seasons provide a natural and magical yearly rhythm for children. Being in touch with nature can bring untold pleasure: a wonder and joy forgotten until we connect back to the Earth, and remember deep inside ourselves the secret wisdom of the seasons.

Observe and share in the miracle of a natural year on Earth with a family seasonal table, craft, outings, and many adventures in the garden and local nature spots. Let your children see and know the wonder of a flower opening and a bird's nest in spring, an autumn leaf falling (Quick! Catch it before it hits the ground!), snow in winter, and the long summer days. Hear the hidden wave sounds in a seashell, and watch a bug with so many legs! The Earth abounds in simple, joyous, natural wonders that enrich the lives of children (and adults too).

The Seasonal Table

A seasonal table is one way for families to connect with the Earth and the natural rhythm of the year. It is a special area inside your house to represent the season and display nature's treasures. Children love to be a part of the creating and changing of a seasonal table.

The seasonal table can use a shelf, small table, or a window ledge. Look for a suitable place in your home; it could be in the centre of your dining room table. If you have nothing suitable, purchase a small secondhand table. (The table won't be seen, once it becomes 'seasonal'!) Next visit a secondhand shop for some vases: little ones for little hands to put flowers in.

Autumn to winter

Coloured Cloths

Place a coloured cloth on the table and perhaps hang another (lighter) cloth from a hook on the wall. These cloths set a soft, beautiful backdrop for this special nature place.

Choose the cloth colours to represent the season. Spring colours include the greens of new grass, and pinks and peaches of blossom. The summer colours are yellows and blues that represent the beach and the bright sun. Autumn colours can be brown, red and orange, the shades of falling leaves. Winter colours may include ice blue for the sky, and dark brown and white for the earth and snow. Add pieces of cotton drill or cord from material stores. Look out for lovely pieces of fabric or tablecloths in secondhand shops. Muslin seasonal cloths and seasonal cards enliven the seasonal table. The scene has been set...

What Else Might You Find for a Seasonal Table?

For spring, place a vase of flowers, blossom branches or flowering bulbs on the table. Blossom fairies and butterflies can be lovingly made to hang on the blossom branches. You'll find ideas and instructions in seasonal craft books. Birds' nests can be placed on the table, as well as toy animals, with their springtime babies. Children will enjoy collecting flowers and blossoms to arrange.

During summer time it is lovely to place a selection of seashells on the table, and maybe some fish in a bowl or some fabric fish in a pretend cloth sea. A vase of summer flowers adds beauty and wonder to the seasonal table.

My personal favourite is autumn. The Earth abounds with nature's gifts: lovely leaves, tree nuts and pieces of interesting wood and bark. Place these on the seasonal table, and hide some gnomes in secret places (to be found by dedicated searchers!).

For the winter seasonal table, arrange bare branches covered with golden cardboard or sewn felt stars to represent the darker evenings.

A seasonal table brings magic into homes and hearts. Children and adults alike 'wake up' to the changing faces of the seasons around them. This can bring a greater love, respect and awe for the natural world on planet Earth. Nature – it's a miracle!

Ages and Stages

Young children tend to play with a seasonal table and it can get quite messy. Keep it simple at this age. Let them collect special treasures (remembering to respect local codes about what should

Celebrating seasons – autumn

and should not be removed from the environment). Your child will need your guidance and help to set up the table. As the child grows older, you may turn your back one day and find that the table has been set. Little fingers have created magic!

Seasonal Stories

A nourishing part of the annual rhythm is reading stories that represent the season to your children. Elsa Beskow is a wonderful author of imaginative and beautiful seasonal stories for children. Read *Ollie's Ski Trip* for winter, *The Flowers' Festival* for spring, *Woody, Hazel and Little Pip* for autumn, and *The Sun Egg* for summer (all Floris Books). For very young children, seek out the four board books by Gerda Muller that introduce the seasons (Floris Books). These wonderful books have detailed illustrations and no text. They are perfect for talking about the pictures with your children, and can be a starting point for undertaking together the seasonal activities depicted in the drawings. Simple seasonal books provide many opportunities to recognise and share the wonders of everyday life. Place a small selection on the seasonal table or in a basket nearby.

Two books that cover all four seasons are *And The Good Brown Earth* by Kathy Henderson (Walker Books) and *A Year on Our Farm* by Penny Matthews and Andrew McLean (Scholastic Australia). For older children, *The Milly, Molly, Mandy* series by Joyce Lankester Brisley (Macmillan) offers chapter books for each season – lovely!

Many nursery tales are ripe for telling in different seasons. Each winter tell children 'The Magic Porridge Pot' and make porridge together: 'Stop little pot, stop!' Winter is the perfect time to hear 'Goldilocks and the Three Bears': make sure you invite the three bears to share breakfast porridge! In springtime, the three Billy Goats Gruff are ready to eat spring grass! After this tale, visit a local farm. Can you spot Great Big Billy Goat Gruff? During spring, the Little Red Hen's wheat is planted and in summer it is ripe. This is a great repetitive story for children (with hidden morals about sharing work).

Seasonal Songs with Actions

Songs match seasons too. In the summer time, toes are exposed! Perfect for 'This Little Piggy'. On the subject of piggies, read 'The Three Little Pigs', then see if houses of straw, sticks and little rock bricks can be built in the garden. 'Oh, I do like to be beside the seaside' is a cheering tune during a car trip to the sea! Autumn songs include falling leaves (and dancing children):

Like a leaf or a feather in the windy, windy weather
We swirl around and twirl around
And all fall down together!

I like to rake the leaves
Into a great big hump,
I now take a big step back
And jump!

Winter songs include 'Here we go Round the Mulberry Bush', which helps with outside winter clothes: 'This is the way we put on our hat/boots/coat on a cold and frosty morning.' 'I Hear Thunder' is good for wet weather and 'Twinkle, Twinkle Little Star' can be sung on darker nights.

In springtime turn to songs about baby birds and animals (nature's wonders). Remember:

Two little dicky birds sitting on a wall,
One named Peter, one named Paul.
Fly away Peter! fly away Paul!
Come back Peter; come back Paul.

Springtime calls for a tune! 'Mary had a Little Lamb' (can you visit baby lambs at a farm?) and 'Five Little Ducks' (spot some baby ducks too).

Seasonal Outings

It is lovely to go on family outings to recognise the Earth's many faces in the seasons. Experiencing the same outing over a period of time through different seasons can develop trust, wonder and a yearly rhythm for your child.

If you live close to snow, go tobogganing in winter. And of course, build a snowman! Go for a morning walk to see where Jack Frost has been.

Find bushes, plants, shrubs and trees flowering in springtime abundance in your local area or at a botanical garden. Spring is the time to visit a farm or to watch nearby farmer's fields; find where the baby animals are hiding.

A trip to the beach is wonderful during summer: making sandcastles and splashing in waves is a joy.

Find your nearest park or botanical gardens with beautiful autumn leaf colours. Catch leaves, play with them and collect special ones for craft activities. Sing the falling leaves song (above)!

Each season has a seasonal outing gift. While on outings, perhaps collect some seasonal offerings you can use in your craft projects back at home.

A Suggestion

Buy an all-in-one wet weather suit for toddlers, a fun child's umbrella and wellies for splashing in puddles! Little ones want to experience the wonders of the great outdoors in every season!

Seasonal Craft

Using nature to create craft can be fun and inspiring for young children. Their craft can then become part of the seasonal table.

In autumn, try leaf rubbings. Turn the leaf over so that the veins are sticking up, and then place a plain piece of paper on top. Rub with crayon and an imprint of the leaf will come through onto the paper – magic! Cut around the crayon paper leaves and hang them on branches in a vase.

Winter craft can include paper snowflakes. Cut a circle around a dinner plate; fold the paper in half (creating a semi-circle), half again and again. You now have a cone shape. Take small scissors and snip little shapes (triangles, half circles, squares) along the folded edges of the paper. Open to find a beautiful snowflake! These can be hung on bare branches or make a backdrop to the seasonal table.

Paper snowflake

When spring is in the air, pick flowers. Place them on greaseproof paper between two heavy telephone books. After a few weeks, open this 'press' up again to find the pressed flowers, now ready to make into a special card or bookmark.

Collect bark and leaves to make little boats in summertime (if you live near eucalyptus trees, their bark and gum leaves are good for this). Push the leaf through a bark bottom boat. Can the boat sail down the river or float in a bucket of water? Find more seasonal craft ideas in the next chapter.

As an adult, before I had children, I was somewhat asleep to the natural world around me. As I celebrated the seasons with my young children, my eyes opened. What joy I now experience at the sight of flowering winter wattle, or autumn leaves falling! It is as if I am seeing the world for the first time, through a child's eyes. Celebrating the seasons is a gift to adults too.

If we enjoy and marvel at the seasons, our children will too. If we understand the healing powers of nature, we take our children to visit her. If our children spend time 'unplugged' in the garden they will come to know the Earth. If family walks are a weekly event (take bikes and snacks to keep little people happy), it means outings feel like a normal part of life. If little feet are tired, tell stories along the way, or play 'I Spy'.

Children experience a quiet inner knowing that they are a part of this big, amazing and miraculous universe.

Something to Try

Plant a fruit tree in the garden, or in a pot, and observe its changes through the seasons. (There are more gardening ideas in the next chapter.)

A Word from a Dad – Michael

Children need to get wet and muddy, and help with gardening chores. What is really most important, getting the job done quickly, or building a relationship with children?

A Word from Seven-year-old Jayson

I love to go to the snow in winter, and in the summer I swim in the river. My sister and I change the seasonal table. Our seasonal table is a window-sill in our porch.

Reflection

Watching and celebrating the four seasons is like the soul's journey through life. The bright summer months shine with joy, expansion and outdoor adventures. Autumn teaches the letting go needed to live life in the moment, and contains the inner knowledge of eternity. The elm and oak are bare, but new life waits, reincarnating. Winter is the time for inner reflection, quiet moments, peace and solitude. Then a new light begins to shine, even in the darkest hours, for spring shouts the glory of new life: a new day and a new beginning.

Real Life Story
Kate – Our Seasonal Table

For several years now, our family has constructed a seasonal display. For a table, we use the top of my great aunt's old wooden Singer sewing machine, in the corner of our lounge. We heard of the idea when my first child was a toddler. I was inspired to create a spot in my home to honour the Earth and all her seasons, and to encourage my children's awareness of the world around them as well.

Our seasonal table consists of a piece of coloured cloth that represents the season. On this may be placed other objects that will bring the season inside. As I write, our spring table is adorned with a beautiful card with a picture of a spring garden, a vase of bare twigs from which hang silk butterflies (made by my six-year-old), a posy of white snowbells (onion weed from the local creek!) and a pink cloth.

The table is not static: often when we are out on our walks or busy in the garden, my four children collect some treasures for the seasonal display. In fact, sometimes we can barely see the wood underneath because the children have so enthusiastically gathered beautiful autumn leaves and conkers, winter wattle, summer abalone shells or spring pussy willow.

Everything gathered is a free gift from nature, and everything is returned, composted or put away for next year's table. The children love it when I put away a special few things and bring them out the following year – they are full of joyful reminiscences: 'Oh, I remember that day at the beach with Nana when there were so many shells that we filled our pockets and our shoes!'

Arranging the table encourages the children to interact with natural objects and builds within them a sense of beauty and design. Creating this spot is so much a part of our lives that I cannot imagine not having a seasonal table now!

Real Life Story
Kate – Camping with my Family

For us, camping is a regular event. Our children began camping when they were each only a few months old and have camped many times a year since then. We love to camp for many reasons. Mostly we just love to get away from civilisation, immerse ourselves in nature and get back to basics. We sleep in an old canvas tent, cook on the fire, haul water from the river, wash in a bucket and go to bed when it is dark. We experience the weather in all its fullness. We love the fact that camping is a cheap family holiday and it can be an easy way for lots of families to plan a holiday together. We also love the skills and confidence it brings to our children. I often think we are teaching our children that all you need is a tent and a sleeping bag and you can make a great, adventurous holiday.

When we camp we sing songs around the fire, the kids whittle sticks, build dams in the creek, climb trees, play imaginary games, bush walk, swim, kayak and eat. Actually, we eat a lot and the food tastes so good when you are living outside. We talk and talk and play games as a family. We really relax in a way that we don't relax on any other holiday – I guess there is something so restorative and healing about just being in the bush.

We always camp in state forests where fires are allowed and prefer if there are very few facilities. As the children have grown we have become more confident in finding new (and even more remote) camping spots. When they were toddlers we wouldn't drive more than two hours and we would only manage to camp for about three nights. After that we were worn out as they never slept as well as at home. But we persevered, and bought them better sleeping mats, and soon the children had grown more and learnt to relax in a tent. We now camp for up to two weeks. We started out in well-known camping grounds and even tried a caravan park (only once – it was too noisy for us). But, our confidence has grown and we now look for camping areas that are difficult to access (4WD or hike in) so that there are fewer people, dogs and trail bikes. Every holiday brings more courage and often in the car on the way home we find ourselves saying, 'Where shall we try next year?' I love the fact that we are getting to know our country, bit by bit.

Checklist – Celebrating the Seasons

1. Find a good location to set up a seasonal table in your home.

2. Share wonderful seasonal stories and songs with your young children.

3. Plan outings to experience the seasons together.

4. Make seasonal craft to put on the seasonal table.

5. Spend time outside every day.

6. Plant a vegetable patch and fruit trees; watch the seasons in the garden.

7. Observe the seasons yourself; they're a wonder!

Chapter Four
Crafty and Clever

Nimble fingers make nimble minds.

The Importance of Craft

When children creatively use their hands, they also work their brains! You've heard about occupational therapists, who give basket-weaving activities to stroke patients? Activities that require finger dexterity invisibly join up neurons and balance both sides of the brain. Young children who engage in fine motor craft activities may well have better handwriting later in life!

Craft not only supports a healthy brain function, it stimulates feelings of wonder in young children, fosters their imagination and gives a settled sense of centeredness. What fun! Confidence and craft go hand in hand: creating brings self-esteem.

Keeping Craft Alive

In our highly technological and busy world – with its predominance of TV, electronic games, and stimulating out-of-home activities – we are losing the art of craft, the healing qualities that quiet doing brings to life. Working the hands calms the mind and nurtures the heart. There are many simple ways to creatively use our hands: everyday life can include creative moments – involve your child in daily cooking and gardening chores. These activities offer the three 'C's to your child: connection, creativity and communication. And life skills!

Crafty and clever

Cooking Pleasures

Cooking is a fun and life-changing activity for children. By inviting children to help create family meals, you ensure they will gain the skills to be cooking your tea when they are nine years old. (No kidding!) And be able to leave home independent and super-skilled for life. A special apron and footstool turn everyday meals into a cooking adventure. If they're interested, children can help with every meal. Can they spread, stir or chop? A weekly rhythm of baking for the biscuit tin is not only fun, but also gives children something to look forward to. Children like to cook special treats for loved ones at Christmas time and other occasions too. Yes, it can be messy, but the rewards are worth it!

Pretzel Dough

One of my favourite activities with children is making pretzel dough. This can become a part of your weekly rhythm.

* 1 tsp yeast
* 120 ml (4 fl oz) warm water
* 1 tsp honey
* 1 tsp salt
* 200 g (7 oz) plain flour
* beaten egg or milk

In a large bowl dissolve 1 tsp of yeast in 120 ml (4 fl oz) of warm water.
Add 1 tsp of honey and 1 tsp of salt.
Add to these 200 g (6 ¾ oz) of plain flour.
Knead the dough, divide into pieces and let children play and make shapes with it.
Place the shapes on to an oiled baking tray and brush lightly with beaten egg or milk.
Bake for 10 minutes in a moderate oven (180° C; 350° F).
Eat warm with butter and jam. Yum!

This is the real play dough: playing with dough!

Tahini Cookies

Tahini cookies are the tastiest and healthiest biscuits. After first finding it in Bonner, Kingsmill and Morrow's *Recipes to the Rescue* (Viking), I have given this recipe to many parents. It involves lots of measuring and stirring for small hands!

* 6 tbs tahini
* 60 g (2 oz) honey
* 1 egg
* 200 g (7 oz) rice flakes (or other cereal, e.g. cornflakes)
* 100g (3½ oz) desiccated coconut
* 100g (3½ oz) sunflower seeds

Mix together tahini and honey. Add remaining ingredients, stirring well. Drop tablespoons of mixture onto a well-greased tray and bake until brown but not overcooked in a moderate oven (180° C; 350° F).

The Magic of Gardening

Include gardening time in your children's life; it's so good for their well-being! A child's wheelbarrow, shovel, gloves, a little watering can and some vegetable seedlings make a great Christmas or birthday present. It is a joy for children to plant, water and harvest.

Creating a Vegetable Garden

The first thing to do when planning your vegetable garden is to consider where it will go. Ideally choose an area that gets a lot of sun (at least five hours a day) and where vegetables will not have to compete for nutrients with the root systems of large trees and shrubs. Once an area is chosen, dig the soil over to the depth of a fork. After digging, if the soil is poor, add compost, organic matter and manure to ensure rich nutrients for the soon-to-be-planted veggies.

Now you are ready to plant! Follow the directions given with the seedlings or on the back of the seed packet, and remember to water them in well. Keep up the water for the first few weeks until the plants have established themselves, then give them a deep soak a couple of times a week.

For ongoing maintenance, keep on top of weeds, as the weeds will compete for nutrients and potentially crowd out your plants.

Gardening fun

Good mulch will help with weed prevention and also keep the water in the soil, where you want it.

A 'No-Dig' Vegetable Garden

If you don't have time to prepare the soil correctly, or don't have a small space, or have to make a garden on concrete, then a no-dig garden may be perfect for you.

If your chosen site is on top of existing lawn, then you will need to mow the grass down as much as possible. If you have chosen a hard surface, such as old paving, you will need to lay some cushioning organic material, such as soil or straw.

To start your no-dig garden, you should lay down a layer of newspaper approximately ½ cm (¼ in) thick. Once you have done this, lay a border around your garden using bricks, wood, rocks or whatever other suitable material you may have, to at least a height of 20-25 cm (8-10 in) to contain the organic material and discourage weeds.

After building the border, put down a layer of Lucerne hay or other type of hay approximately 10 cm (4 in) thick. On top of this, layer some good organic fertiliser or manure to a thickness of 2½ cm (1 in). A 15 cm (6 in) thick layer of loose straw should then be laid, followed by another layer of fertilizer and then finished off with a 10 cm (4 in) thick layer of compost.

Now that this is done, just water the garden thoroughly. You can then start planting!

Spinach Sausage Rolls

There are so many different vegetables and herbs to choose from, depending on your climate, tastes and the time of year (gain specific advice from your local nursery).

It can work well to grow some green leafy vegetables together. Here is a recipe for Spinach Sausage Rolls, which uses spinach, parsley and mint. These are all relatively easy to grow in the garden or in pots, and will be happy in a variety of climatic conditions.

* 8–10 big spinach or chard or silverbeet leaves, washed
* small bunch of parsley, washed, and chopped finely (optional)
* 8–10 mint leaves, washed, and chopped finely (optional)
* 1 onion, chopped finely
* olive oil
* nutmeg

- ✻ ground pepper
- ✻ 100 g (3½ oz) feta cheese
- ✻ 100 g (3½ oz) ricotta cheese
- ✻ pastry (homemade, or purchase sheets of puff pastry – fresh or frozen)

Fry the onion gently in olive oil. Cut the stems off the spinach or chard or silverbeet, and finely chop. Add all the finely chopped greens and herbs to the onion. Continue to cook gently, turning occasionally, until spinach leaves have wilted and the whole lot is reduced. Allow to cool.

Crumble feta and ricotta into a large bowl. Sprinkle with nutmeg and pepper. Add the onion and greens. Mix well. (I often put the whole lot in the blender for a quick whiz – this can make the next bit easier.)

Defrost a sheet of frozen pastry and cut into 4 rectangular pieces (or make the pastry, roll it out, and cut into rectangles). Form a sausage-shape of the cheese-and-greens mix parallel with the narrow end of the rectangle, about 1½ cm (½ inch) in from the end. Start rolling that end of the pastry over the mixture. Wet the outside of the pastry with water to help it stick, and roll right over. Prick the top of the pastry.

This quantity of greens mixture is enough for 8 rolls (that is, enough to fill rectangles cut from 2 sheets of pastry). Cook according to the pastry instructions (about 20 minutes at 200° C (375° F) in my oven).

Allow the rolls to cool slightly before handling, and eating. Delicious!

To plant, water, watch and wait, harvest and then cook – magical!

Something to Try

Place unused soft toy animals around the veggie patch. They make terrific rabbit and possum frighteners.

Something to Try

Each autumn and early winter, plant spring bulbs in a pot or in the garden. This is a satisfying gardening activity for children and the surprise in springtime is wonderful to witness together.

Woodwork

Another great activity for children outside in the garden is working with wood. They can sandpaper sawn branches to make blocks, or hammer nails into an old tree stump (under your supervision). This will develop skills and interests that will be handy when they are older.

Buy children's tool belts so they are dressed to impress! Let children watch tradespeople doing big things; they are usually taking everything in.

My husband and our son built a cubby house using recycled materials. It was my husband's first project, and I don't know who learnt more, or had the most fun! If this is too big an idea, buy a wooden toy car or boat kit to make together.

Drawing Equipment

Be aware when you are choosing drawing tools to be used by young children that at first they will be bitten and chewed! Matching art equipment to children's ages and stages really makes a difference. Felt-tip pens are made of plastic, which is environmentally unsustainable. They also dry out easily, which leads to frustration. Further, a young child's grip is not yet sufficiently developed for holding a thin pen or pencil correctly. Crayons are better.

The best crayons I have used are Stockmar crayons. They are rectangular-block shaped, come in a range of pure colours, are made from beeswax and are totally non-toxic. The block shape is cleverly versatile: the long side (Sideward Sam) shades easily, while the point (Peter Pointer) can be used to draw lines. The rich, pure colours and the beeswax smell on fingertips are uplifting for children – and for their drawings! Crayons made of petrochemical oils and emulsifiers are a poor substitute.

Art is not about drawing perfect pictures; it is about experiencing colour and movement. All children scribble in spirals and circles. A child's drawing of a person develops slowly, in his or her own unique time. Sitting next to children and drawing pictures for them to copy may lead to children stating that your picture is better than theirs (and that they cannot draw). Children observe the world around them and draw from their own experience and imagination. Focus on the experience of the process rather than an outcome. Children love to experiment. In all craft pursuits, give perfection a miss: aim for enjoyment. The joy of truly creating!

Keep crayons and paper in a basket and, from time to time throughout the week, put the basket on the table in a fun and easy family rhythm. By leaving art equipment out permanently, walls may well get drawn on!

If you have a paved area, it's fun to draw outside using big chalk. It washes off easily in the rain.

Set up painting from time to time. In the warmer months, use an easel outside.

Meaningful Craft: Seasonal Ideas

A significant memory from my time as a young schoolgirl is of my weekly craft sessions: I did basket weaving, and made a bird-table out of wood. I remember the feeling of anticipation waiting for my next craft session, and my joy at working magic with my hands compared to academic work. As parents, we can bring that joy to our children, and back into our own lives.

Look for craft ideas that will produce an object that might last the test of time, rather than something that will end up broken in the bin or forgotten soon after it's finished.

When choosing activities, natural treasures are special craft resources that inspire young children. Reflecting the season in your choices can also help render craft more immediately meaningful.

Wonderful seasonal craft books include: (my absolute favourite) *Earthwise: Environmental Crafts and Activities* by Carol Petrash (Floris Books); *The Children's Year* by Stephanie Cooper, Christine Fynes-Clinton and Marye Rowling (Hawthorn Press); and *The Big Summer Activity Book* by Anne and Peter Thomas (Floris Books).

Little gumnut or acorn people and leaf crowns are fun to make in autumn. In winter, it's lovely to work with wool, like making a pom-pom. A pine-kernel bird feeder is a good idea in the colder months. The springtime wind plays with handmade kites or ribbon wands. In summer, try paper boats for little hands.

You need never feel that you are not 'crafty'; it's fun to learn alongside our children. Buy a book and choose one or two craft activities a season to enjoy together. Keep materials in a special craft basket.

Easy Bird Feeder

Here is a favourite craft activity for winter. I've adapted it from one in *Earthwise: Environmental Crafts and Activities*, by Carol Petrash (Floris Books). Children of all ages can participate in this.

You will need:

* A pine cone, or a branch, or even an empty toilet roll will do;
* A tray or large plate or bowl;
* A piece of string or wool;
* Lolly or craft sticks or butter knives to spread with;
* Peanut butter or, if there may be allergies to peanuts, honey;
* Bird seed;

First tie a loop of string or wool onto your pine cone, branch or toilet roll. It can be messy to do this later! Next spread the pine cone, branch or toilet roll with peanut butter or honey. Tip the birdseed onto the tray or plate or into the bowl and roll the pine cone, branch or toilet roll in it until covered. Find a tree to tie the bird feeder on – one that can be seen from a window. Wait and watch: the birds will nibble your feeder clean, and then you can coat it again.

Craft Kits

There are wonderful craft kits available that use wood, paper and wool, and also kits to make soaps, candles, paper flowers and wooden cars. I always try to include a craft kit in my children's Christmas stockings. My family can then spend time creating, communicating and connecting together during the Christmas break.

The Gift of Giving!

In this fast-paced, commercialised world, people love to receive homemade gifts. When young children make their own presents and cards for special people in their lives they get to enjoy giving as well as receiving. Easy ideas include: baking biscuits and cakes; making your own wrapping paper out of children's paintings; creating cards from drawings and pressed flowers. Christmas is a great time to involve your children in making homemade cards and small gifts. Time for craft before a loved one's birthday is also worthwhile. Craft doesn't have to take long – it can be quicker to make a card than popping to the shops for a bought one!

Perfecting Patience

Craft can push buttons, too! Glue doesn't stick, or the end result doesn't look like the picture on the box. Crafts can be a good means to learn patience and resilience! Remember it is the process, not the end product, that counts. Who wants perfection, when it is made with love?

Appropriate Ages

At a young age, small children are able to watch their parents make the craft kit or craft activity and help where they can. As they get older, they can become more and more involved and inspired to create, and to follow the instructions themselves. An adult displaying a love for cooking, craft and gardening is an important role model. Adult craft can include making homemade toys for children. It is inspiring for both the adult and child to see the process and then the completion. Parents who value craft create crafty children.

Adults and Craft

Craft is healing and inspiring for adults too. My husband – an accountant – talks to top businessmen who quietly admit that they have always wanted to work with wood, or on some hands-on creative project. When I started to sew felt animals and dolls for my children, I thought I was not crafty or artistic at all, but I found that I could not stop! My husband used to call himself a 'sewing widower'! Craft became like a meditation to me; it was centering and grounding. Craft can be compared to alchemy: at first there is nothing, and then something appears for the first time in the world. It is time put to good creative use.

Knitting and Sewing

If a member of your family knows how to knit, it is possible to knit a whole farmyard of little animals – for hours of farmyard play. Encourage this person to teach children of seven years or older how to knit – boys as well, please. Knitting is very good for firing up and balancing the young child's brain. Here's a rhyme that might help explain a knitting stitch: 'In through the rabbit hole, around the big tree, out through the rabbit hole and away ran he!' Visit the local library to find simple knitting patterns for making children's toys.

You can sew felt toys while children are playing, and in the evening. Children love the results. All it takes is blanket stitch, and away you go! All farm animals and simple dolls can be made with this stitch: refer to Petra Berger's wonderful book, *Feltcraft: Making Dolls and Gifts and Toys* (Floris Books).

For children, a little sewing kit is fun. Use hessian material: it comes with holes in it, which makes sewing much easier. Buy special blunt needles with a big eye, so wool, instead of cotton, can be used. Your young child is now ready to sew around the shape of a fish or animal. These homemade toys can live in the play corner.

Have you considered mosaics? Maybe buy a book and visit the local tile shop.

What creative pursuit do you enjoy?

> ## *Reflection*
>
> How does Grandma feel when given a gift made by a child?

Making Cards

When we are out in nature, I take photos of beautiful scenes. I turn these pictures into cards for birthdays and other celebrations. My children like to choose the photo to use for each special occasion.

There are many ways to make homemade cards. Here's an idea for creating moving-picture cards your children can enjoy each year. Draw a simple background on a piece of card; then, on another piece, draw an animal or object that moves. Cut out this small picture and stick it to a twig or lolly stick. Cut a slit in the background card and poke the small moving picture on a stick through the slit. You have a wonderful moving-picture birthday card. Imagine how children feel if they are made a moving birthday card each year? The anticipation builds! What will my moving picture be this year?

A moving-picture card

Crafty Rhythm

Try to go along with your child's interests; notice what they love. My son really enjoys cooking, my daughter enjoys craft, and both enjoy gardening. Setting a time to do craft each week can work wonders. If you, say, structure your week with the intention to do craft on Mondays, then the weeks (and months and years) will not pass by without you being 'crafty and clever' together. Including craft for our children does not have to take a lot of time. Through craft, children become creators in and of their world.

A word from a Dad – Michael

I was about four or five and it was a rare time: my dad was at home, making a garden bench. I was in awe of his power and skill; he drove the nails effortlessly. This was a bench, it was in the ground, and it was forever!

A Word from Seven-year-old Jayson

I like cooking pasta, pizza, curries and cakes. I came up with the idea of building a veggie patch. I have grown lots of lettuce, parsley, rocket and spinach.

Real Life Story

Helen – Our Patchwork Quilt

I was given my nan's old sewing machine after she passed away. My nan loved to sew little dolly's clothes and all sorts of craft. It sat in my cupboard for over two years. One day I became inspired. A local patchwork quilt shop had opened in my area. I loved the quilts and I now had a sewing machine. I studied a simple square pattern, then took my son to choose material (printed with cars, planes and trains, of course). I even bought the equipment to cut and measure material – I was serious!

The sewing machine came out of the cupboard. It was an old, reliable, basic model, with a history of my Nan's hands. My son and I looked at it in amazement. I showed him the foot pedal, which soon became the 'hand' pedal: he pressed down on it. I shouted 'Go!' and he pressed as I sewed. We worked together. It took over a year to sew the squares together. We went at our own pace!

I then asked myself, 'Will it take another two years to sew the patchwork into a quilt?' No. I visited the shop again and got the number of a business that stuffs quilts!

I was embarrassed when I took our handmade, wobbly, imperfect quilt along. I quickly explained it was made by a six-year-old! They thought it was great, even though they had to tape some parts together with sticky tape before sewing. I admired the perfect quilts on the walls.

The day arrived: we received a phone call saying to

come and pick up our finished quilt. We went after school, and it was amazing to see our vision finally complete. Since then the quilt has lived on my son's bed. I know his less-than-perfect quilt is perfect. It wraps him warmly at night. It holds the memories of our creative time together: my son on the 'hand' pedal while I steered the way! He aptly calls it his 'love blanket'.

Checklist – Crafty and Clever

1. Understand that craft is important: it is great for the brain and the heart!

2. Do you have a creative activity that *you* enjoy?

3. Everyday cooking can be craft time with your child. (They love a special apron!)

4. Buy a book of seasonal craft ideas.

5. Choose crayons carefully. (See my advice above.)

6. Leave your child free to draw their own pictures.

7. Make special cards and gifts for loved ones with your child.

8. Make special cards and gifts for your child.

9. Purchase craft kits for birthday and Christmas presents.

10. Involve your child in all your creative adventures, if they are interested. If *you* are interested, they most probably will be!

11. Can you plant a garden or even some herbs in pots?

12. A little wheelbarrow and gardening spade are wonderful toys for a child.

13. Create a crafty weekly rhythm in your home.

Chapter Five
Once Upon a Time...

If you want your children to be intelligent, read them fairy tales. If you want your children to be more intelligent, read them more fairy tales.

ALBERT EINSTEIN

Just Tell Stories

A chef friend of mine wants to write a cookbook called *Just Cook!* I think this title is great: simple and to the point. Likewise, I introduce this chapter with the heading 'Just tell stories!'

For children, the best stories are the ones that you make up yourself. These made-up stories are truly alive with imagination. Please do not worry: it's like singing lullabies, you need no previous experience. Just give it a go, that's all.

Stories can be spontaneous: if a little bird appears in a tree in your garden, make up a story about his home and life. When the cat comes in after a day outside, what has he been doing? Tell stories when the mood and inspiration takes you. It is fun to have a special family theme, one that is unique to your children – maybe about a rabbit or a sweet songbird from your garden.

Choose a theme that inspires your child. My son had stories about a rubbish truck for a while – they soothed him! He had been frightened of rubbish trucks, and giving them a friendly face through storytelling helped. In general, do not create scary stories, and choose something from the natural world, such as an animal, to focus on. This connects children to the Earth and its many wonders. A dog is a trusted companion. In my family, our regular story character is a dog called Bingo (my children had sung the song about Bingo the dog at school).

Bingo has entertained my children on long car journeys and tiring walks. He has helped to heal their hearts when they are upset or scared. He has made them laugh, helped them to count (he lives on a farm and there are lots of things to plant on a farm!) and he displays lovely qualities like good manners and respect for all people and the Earth. He walked alongside their childhood, making it magical and full of surprises. He is a childhood friend. And yes, he is a story, an ongoing one, with many parts.

How to Become a Story Teller

It's easy: just begin! Keep the beginning of the story the same each time. This provides safety, anticipation and enjoyment, 'On the farm each morning Farmer Jo's alarm clock went off at seven o'clock. Bingo reached out his left paw and hit the snooze button...' I usually start with a general theme in my head, and then go with the flow. I often choose a theme by copying the actual events or issues affecting children at the time.

If we are going to a festival, Bingo is in a parade at a festival. If we are busy cooking, Bingo is helping farmer Josephine cook for the market stall. Bingo stories are very useful if children are feeling anxious – amazingly Bingo is feeling the same thing. A little moral creeps in from time to time: how Bingo learnt to share or to treat the sheep kindly. Let me emphasise, when I tell stories, I have no idea where the story is going. I start with a general theme and see where it leads. The children often call out and add to the story along the way, because it is alive and magical.

As children grow older, play the car game of telling a story together, each family member giving one line at a time.

Tell stories: they are free, and connect us together. Candlelight is a magical atmosphere for stories. It can be fun to put on a special cloak, hat or scarf each time we tell a story at home, before the bedtime rhythm. This may give us confidence to put on a 'storytelling' role.

Enriching Experiences

As with singing a lullaby, children are more enriched by your stories than anything already written in a book or anything pre-recorded. They hear your voice, feel your inventiveness and are wrapped in your connection to them. When the story is made up on the spot, creativity is in the air! Our own imaginations make all the pictures in our heads: this is an inspiring moment. Telling a story teaches children the skills to develop their own stories – a useful tool when they study English language at school. We are being role models they can later imitate.

When I was a Child...

Another story that children love to hear is 'When I was your age...' They enjoy listening to our childhood adventures. This type of story is very useful if children are worried, or if something unpleasant has happened to them. For example, 'Did you know when I was a little girl I cut my knee? I cried and there was a lot of blood but Mummy gave me a plaster and drew a picture on it with a pen, and that made me feel better. Shall I draw one on your plaster too?'

In our extended families we have ample storytelling material. Encourage Grandpa and Nana to tell of their lives and adventures as children.

Birth and Childhood Stories

Children love to hear loving stories of their birth, how their parents felt when they first saw them, and their baby adventures. 'When you were a baby, you...' This again provides many moments of connection, communication, and creativity together, and is an important storytelling tool when a new sibling is born. Each time the baby does something new, tell a story about the older child at the same age: 'When you were a baby and first started to roll, you went right off the mat and across this floor! What a wonderful roller you were.' This helps to prevent sibling jealousy.

Stories to Teach and Comfort

Stories are very useful if you would like to put a point across. An incident may have happened in the day but, rather than deal with it in the heat of the moment, you might wait and tell a story about it later, including in the story what could happen to make amends. For instance: 'When I was a little girl, I found it really hard to share with my sister. One day, our mother bought us a special timer with a duck on it. We wound the duck around to ten minutes, and then instead of arguing we each took a turn with the toy while the duck ticked. I loved this little game; we learnt to take turns with our duck friend! Shall I buy a special timer for you two, too?' Storytelling is a handy tool to have in the parenting toolbox!

'Trying Moments'

When little voices are saying 'Are we there yet?', tell stories in the car, or try them when sibling squabbles have started. Tell stories on a walk so little feet will forget they are walking. Tell a story at that point in the day when your child needs to slow down and rest. Stories are useful parenting tools to change the atmosphere and shift a child's mood. (And our mood too!)

Imaginative Story Games

Create a 'let's pretend' story to change the mood when you're all in a hurry: 'We are cheetahs moving fast, not snails slithering along the grass. Come on, be a cheetah with me!' 'Has the forklift arrived for pack-away time?' Lift the child's hand up and place it on the toys, then press a pretend button to drive the 'forklift' back to the shelf! How about, 'The horses gallop to their bedroom stable!' These little 'story' games work!

Storytelling with Props

Can you make a magical scene on the carpet with your children's play cloths, farm animals and people? Now weave a story around the scene. Well-known stories can be told in a floor play, in front of sparkling eyes. Adults performing stories with props in this way encourage creative play in children. Children imitate over time, setting up scenes and making up little stories by themselves, developing their play, imagination, language and storytelling skills.

In a child's play corner, include: coloured play cloths (particularly green and blue for land and water), wooden blocks (for houses, walls and bridges), pine cones and unusually-shaped wooden pieces (for trees and trolls), wooden animals and people; and an array of natural objects. I have seen 'The Three Billy Goats Gruff' told using different sized pine cones for the goat family and a funny-shaped bit of wood for the troll. Not one child said 'That isn't a goat, it's a pine cone!' They were all imagining the story; it was alive and real to them.

When you decide to tell a story with props, it can be lovely to keep the props inside a basket. Then children can unpack and tell the story themselves, especially once they've seen an adult tell it a few times.

Reading Story Books

Create a daily rhythm for your storybook time. Children like the predictability of this special connecting part of each day. 'Story time' does not necessarily have to be at bedtime; a lullaby is a softer option, or sing after reading one story. Too many story images can replay in the children's head before sleep, or become overly stimulating. Instead, books can be shared in the morning, when you snuggle in your big bed together, at rest time after lunch, or while children are eating an afternoon snack. For me, now that my children are at school, the best time to read to them is when they get home, before tea, on the sofa. It is the way we unwind, relax and connect together. Hop onto your big bed to share a tale.

Story play

Story time

Repetition

Children love to hear the same story, over and over and over again! Variety is not always the spice of life. They may request the same story every day for three weeks before asking for a change. It is important to avoid saying, 'We had that story yesterday, let's choose a different one.' The deep absorption of a story enabled by repeated readings is very beneficial to children. It also gives the measure of a story. If I can read a book over and over again without pulling my hair out, it is a good book. It has 'soul power'.

Choosing Books?

Which types of books nurture, inspire and heal? The same guidelines for choosing toys can be used when considering children's books. Does this book show my child an interesting, good and kind world to live in? Does it allow my child's imagination to flourish? Sometimes children's books contain adult humour to keep the adult entertained too. Is this good for a small child? Books by Elsa Beskow are wonderful.

Books without words often include beautiful illustrations and create opportunities to talk about the pictures together – to make up your own stories. As children grow older, books that feature nature, animals, seasons and daily life are good for stimulating conversation about the real world around us. This is your chance to plant sustainable seeds early on, through beautiful books. A love of the Earth in a young child leads to respect of the Earth as an adult!

My son did love his 'around the farm' and 'diggers' books too; all children will have their particular favourite topics. But we can ensure they see a wide variety of story and fairy books.

Don't pack up books or give them away, thinking that your children are now too old for them. Beloved first picture books make great first 'readers' for children once they are learning to read themselves, and they can be kept for the next generation.

If you see a book in a secondhand book shop that will be suitable for your child once they're older, buy it right then: you may not find it again.

Nursery Rhyme Magic

Young children benefit from the language rhythms in nursery rhymes and stories. A traditional nursery rhyme book is highly recommended for your child's library. Many of these rhymes can be acted out on your knee – horse rides in particular! For the under-fives, a collection of traditional stories is a wonderful gift. Tales such as 'The Three Little Pigs', 'Goldilocks and the Three Bears', 'The Little Red Hen', 'The Giant Turnip', 'The Gingerbread Man', and others like these, hold a special quality and magic for children, which is why we never forget them and they have been passed down from one generation to the next!

In such tales the characters go through the ups and downs of life and win through in the end. Each holds a message for living, woven into the magic of the story. They function as guideposts for life, even though no explaining is necessary. Collections of these traditional stories are a wonderful gift for every young child.

Classic stories and songs can be woven into family life. Include traditional rhymes in a daily rhythm for your child, such as a horse ride to bed with actions (a child's horse goes slowly, Mummy or Daddy's horse goes faster and a race horse goes...). There is always time in the day for a tickle game: round and round the garden, like a teddy bear, one step and two steps, and tickly under there!

Try telling a tale during baking time: share the tale of 'The Gingerbread Man' before making gingerbread, or sing 'The Muffin Man' while mixing up muffins.

Tip

Avoid or minimise reliance on electronic stimuli (TV and electronic games), and reading and play will flourish! If you are busy, try recorded book readings rather than TV at rest time.

Chapter Books

Between four and five years old, introduce chapter books to children. Chapter books require children to imagine, because they have few pictures. Instead, scenes are created in the child's mind while you read. If you have story time each afternoon as a resting rhythm, the next chapter to the story is much anticipated, and enjoyment maximised.

Buy or make a special book mark – a lovely gum leaf or large feather will do – open the page, take a deep breath, begin...

In our house my children's favourites have included: the *Mr. Galliano's Circus* series, *Billy Bob Tales*, *The Children of Willow and Cherry Tree Farm*, *Tales of Toyland* and *Naughty Amelia Jane* (Enid Blyton); *Milly Molly Mandy* (Joyce Lankester Brisley); *Teddy Robinson* (Joan Robinson); *My Naughty Little Sister* series (Dorothy Edwards); *Mrs Pepperpot* series (Alf Proyson).

I found *The Faraway Tree* series (Enid Blyton) suitable for my children from seven. They enjoyed the simpler Enid Blyton books listed above at an earlier age. For older children (nine onwards), Enid Blyton's *The Famous Five* series has been a favourite with my son, and *Little House in the Big Wood* series (Laura Ingalls Wilder) with my daughter. Also, *Charlie and the Chocolate Factory* and *James and the Giant Peach* (Roald Dahl), *Charlotte's Web* (E.B White), *Heidi* (Johanna Spyri) and *The Secret Garden* (Frances Hodgson Burnett) are wonderful classics.

I do not know who enjoyed these books more, my children or me! As children improve in reading, take it in turns to read a page each, at times: share these classic tales together.

Let your child hear or read classic stories, so they create the imaginative pictures in their own minds. Popular classic books and fairy tales have been made into movies; if the movie is shown first, the movie images will replay when a child is exposed to the written tale (not the child's own imagination). The book is always so much better than the movie! Let children create their own story images, not the movie director's. Their own will be much more powerful and satisfying for their imagination.

The old classics are enthralling stories and can in fact help children sleep at night, as the archetypal people and everyday scenes speak to them about the world and comfort them. The depth of the stories and the wonderful writing style are rarely achieved today. They are called 'classics' for a reason.

Something to Try

Use storytelling to lighten the mood while doing repetitive activities like getting dressed or cleaning teeth. Items of clothing can tell stories. 'I am Sammy Sock, and I love to keep your toes warm. Please let me warm your toes! Do you know where I have been…?' Similarly, the toothbrush can be a story teller (see 'Teethy Tales' in Chapter One).

Real Fairy Tales

Many parents today are unfamiliar with real fairy tales, having grown up with Disney versions or edited books. Fairy tales are crystal jewels of value for children; they tell of overcoming obstacles in life, and moving towards goodness. Some parents think they are not 'nice' reads, as they can include violent incidents and images. But if they are told in a way that does not accentuate negative, loud or scary voices for the characters, and if you limit your comments ('Oh, that was not nice!'), children, deep in their soul, know it is just a story. Hearing a story is quite different from watching it on a screen, as the images are the children's own creation. They are comforted by the archetypes of goodness and the happyily-ever-after ending.

The Brothers Grimm are the most renowned tellers of fairy tales. The two German brothers collected the oral stories told there in the early nineteenth century. Not many people could write, so the oral culture was rich and was handed on with care. These wise old tales date back many centuries. Grimm tales recommended for under-fives include 'Sweet Porridge', 'The Elves and the Shoemaker' and 'The Wolf and the Seven Kids'. Save the rest until the child is over five. *An Illustrated Treasury of Grimms' Fairy Tales* (Floris Books) is a wonderful resource.

Read the fairytales beforehand, to help you choose ones you feel comfortable sharing with children. The wealth in fairy tales is not fully understood by the mind, only in children's hearts and their soul life.

A Love of Reading

Everyone has an innate ability to tell stories. Humans have been telling stories around campfires for thousands of years.

Read often to children, tell made-up-on-the-spot stories, keep high quality books on their shelves, and be seen to read yourself, and they are likely to love reading too. The foundation for a love of reading is reading or telling stories to young children each and every day.

A Word from a Dad – Michael

Every time children play with a dolly or with a car on a car mat, they are telling a story. Engaging with children can be as simple as watching them play and giving them feedback about what they are doing.

Real Life Story
Ally – Telling stories to my children

When asked about the importance of oral story telling within our family, I am immediately transported back into the vivid images created in my mind by my mother's life story. She lived in a small, remote village in northern Greece and her day-to-day experiences were so very different to mine. My early life was filled with tales of her travelling solo through mountain passes full of wild bears, trading bread with German soldiers to survive, and celebrating pagan festivals to ward off evil spirits at harvest time.

Many years later, I visited her tiny village with my mother and my children. I was amazed and overwhelmed to discover how much of the place pulsed through my veins and how in tune I had always been with its rhythms. Her storytelling had filled my already vivid imagination with a vast sense of belonging to a much bigger picture, and with the rich tapestry of life experience, woven through generations of joy, adventure, struggle and sorrow.

Now I see my children wide-eyed when we relate our impressions of life, both lived and imagined. I rediscover the joy of storytelling as I watch expressions play across their faces and see how events unfold in their own lives. I see, too, how they are becoming storytellers through their play and their life encounters. I feel such joy in knowing that we have picked up the thread of this ancient tradition and that we are adding a new texture and colour to enrich future generations.

Real Life Story

Ged – Grandpa's Bedtime Story

Forgetting my young son's books for bedtime was a blessing in disguise. We were visiting Nana and Grandpa's for a sleepover. My wife and I were going out and Grandpa would be putting my son to bed. 'No worries', I said, 'just tell him a story about when you used to drive buses in Malta.' This true tale turned out to be much better than any book from home – my young son was enthralled. My dad, too, was secretly pleased to share some of his own life. I must remember to forget books more often!

Checklist – Once Upon a Time...

1. Just tell stories! Make them up there and then.

2. Develop a theme or character as a base for family stories.

3. Tell a spontaneous story if an animal or bird appears in the window.

4. Use themes that entertain, heal and inadvertently teach. Include topics from children's everyday life.

5. 'When I was a child...'

6. Need to make a point? Tell a story!

7. Tell children's birth stories and baby adventures; they love to hear about their own lives.

8. Make up a little puppet play with children's toys.

9. Collect treasures from nature and coloured cloths to add to farmyard and real life scenes.

10. Remember repetition is fine. 'Read that story again to me!'

11. Before you buy or borrow a book, consider, does it inspire an interesting life of wonder, joy and kindness? Could you read it over and over again?

12. Have you got books that will help to develop a love of the Earth?

13. Include beautifully illustrated books.

14. Have nursery rhyme and nursery story treasuries on the shelf. Every home needs them.

15. Keep their children's books for them to read themselves when they are older.

16. Introduce classic chapter books when children are between four and five years – they are a real gem! Set up a rest time afternoon rhythm with a new chapter each day.

17. Look for books in secondhand shops (all the old classics are out there to collect).

18. Share the power of fairy tales.

Chapter Six
Play – The Best Start

The most effective kind of education is that a child
should play among lovely things.

PLATO

The best start to life for children is to imitate the world around them imaginatively through play. True imaginative play is only possible during childhood. As adults, we can pretend that a block of wood is soap; for a child, the block of wood *is* soap. Pure imagination is a special gift for a short time – for the first ten years of life. Let's make sure children experience 'childhood'.

Given the right environment, play for children is as natural as breathing; it is the basis for their overall development, including social and language skills, problem solving and maths. During play, children use their imaginations to create a world from within themselves. If they have many opportunities to play, they are flexing their cognitive muscles (so to speak), and will become creative thinkers for life.

When considering child's play, the three key words to remember are *imitation*, *imagination* and *movement*. These three impulses run constantly through a child's brain. They are the foundation to childhood and the keys to becoming human.

The Power of Imitation

Children's brains are wired to imitate the human life around them. In *The Spiritual Ground of Education*, Rudolf Steiner explains:

> The whole life of a child up to his seventh year is
> a continuous imitation of what takes place in his
> environment. The moment a child perceives something,
> whether a movement or sound, there arises the impulse
> in him or an inward gesture to re-live what has been
> perceived, with the whole intensity of his nature.

The word 'play' can mean children's play, and it can also mean what is performed in a theatre – a story told by actors on a stage. Yet these two meanings are connected. The true nature of children's play can be likened to a play in the theatre: there is no stage, but it involves experiencing life through taking on roles (imitation). The roles may include a shopkeeper, mummy or daddy, doctor, train driver or farmer. Cars or small animals or dolls might be props or help the child act out a situation. This is fundamental to the wonder and uniqueness of childhood, and is, yes, preparation for adult life!

The Importance of Movement

When they are playing naturally, children move, and their brain neurons develop.

Make sure play has a special place and time in your homes. Think about which toys nurture a child's imagination (their divergent thinking), and which ones might assist their drive to imitate the world around them and learn key human skills. Consider also how to enable their bodily movement. Combine all three – imagination, imitation and movement – and you have a wonderful play environment for growing children.

In these days of iThings (iPhone, iPod, iPad), the three 'i's' of childhood still remain: iMagination, iMitation and the iMpulse to move! These are what are vital for children.

Adult Work is Child's Play

Adult work is child's play. Children love to imitate their parents' actions and imagine keeping house. The negative weight we might feel around chores and housework does not exist for a young child. Daily activities abound in play opportunities, and having a child alongside may brighten your sense of housework too!

Washing up is a wonder to a small child, with bubbles and water. Pull up a chair and give them the spoons and non-breakable items to wash. Cut the dish sponge in half for smaller hands and use environmentally-friendly, non-toxic washing-up liquid. They do get wet, little actual washing-up may get done, the floor will need a mop after, but relax – pop them in the bath or into their pyjamas – we have a happy child and a clean floor! If you have a dishwasher, don't forget to fill the sink from time to time too.

Children delight in helping you cook. A small chopping board and butter knife are all they need. Children can do some of the chopping and grating; their little hands are perfect for slicing mushrooms and bananas. A cook's apron is good: dress for the job! This cooking is not necessarily a special time set aside for including children; it can be part of every day, every meal, when your child is interested.

Make home tasks fun and not tedious, and little hands will want to join in. This not only provides imaginative and imitative play, but good habits, connection time together and life skills. While sorting a washing basket together, colour and size concepts flow easily: 'Can you find the blue sock? Where is the big t-shirt?' These are opportunities to converse naturally, to look into your children's eyes, to share experiences.

Remember the saying:

Tell me and I forget,
Show me and I understand,
Include me and I will remember.

Imitating life

How to Include Children Every Day

Do you have a broom and dustpan and brush in the corner of your kitchen? Perhaps place miniature ones beside them.

Do you carry washing to a clothes horse or line? Find a little basket for tiny socks and pants and set up a low washing line.

After bringing in the dry clothes, let children help sort them into daddy bear, mummy bear and baby bear piles! Also match socks: where is the other blue one hiding?

The weekly shopping can be made fun by taking a little basket for your child, who can be asked to find a special piece of fruit.

A spray bottle and little watering can are handy when you are caring for plants.

A wooden trolley or a special mailbag can be part of a young child's job of collecting the mail each day.

When children are at a loose end, invite them to join in your tasks. When children ask to help, answer 'Yes' as often as possible. They may not be asking so readily when they are teenagers! These real-life skills are fun for children and involving them makes our days together special in little ways.

Children imitate moods, as well as actions; perhaps we can learn to enjoy household chores and cooking for their sake! In *Understanding Waldorf Education* (Floris Books), Jack Petrash says:

> Young children imitate far more than we imagine, and
> the impressions that they take in and mimic become
> behaviours that are learnt for life.

Playing with Boxes

Cardboard boxes are wonderful toys. When you buy a toy from the shop, children may well play more with the cardboard box it came in! So, when you happen to have a box, hang onto it. Small boxes can be made into pretend letterboxes around the house or garden. The postperson is coming! Medium-sized boxes can be made into dog kennels, dolly beds and train carriages. Large ones (never throw them out!) can become toy ovens, boats, castles, all sorts! Try them out in the sandpit, the garden, or with craft materials. Now is the time for imagination to run wild, so get sticky tape and scissors and make box creations. Boxes are kind to the wallet, the environment and our children's imaginations!

The Natural World – Developing Wonder and Awe

Nature provides children with an array of play objects, for free! Look around, start gathering. Feathers make wonderful pretend pens, hair brushes and, in the sandpit, sand cake candles. Gumnuts, acorns and pine cones can be wonderfully transformed in pretend cooking. Shells are perfect for toy money and pretend pasta. Fallen branches can be sawn and made into blocks – small for farms and big for castle walls. As children hold these precious items in their hands, they can feel the secrets and love of nature in their play – priceless!

Recommended Imaginative Play Toys

The toys in this list suit children between the ages of two and seven. Many of these items can be made from recycled goods or from items found around the house. Many can also be picked up from secondhand shops.

A play kitchen

Play stoves can be made out of old bedside cabinets: glue on cork mats for the stove top, and screw wooden door knobs onto a backboard for the dials. An old washing-up bowl can be the sink. Equip the kitchen with small baskets, old small pots, wooden bowls, shells, gumnuts, pine cones, brown bags, cut-up newspaper, old table cloths and doilies, spoons, old kitchen equipment, egg cartons, little bottles, an apron, a wooden dresser.

A tea set

Little espresso cups can be found in secondhand shops. Look also for a small metal teapot.

Dress ups

Collect wooden necklaces, bags of all kinds, old shawls, fairy wings, old shoes, sunglasses, old sunhats, as well as purpose-made children's costumes, which you might find in secondhand shops.

Dolly play

Props might include simple dolls, dolls' clothes, pretend nappies (cut old toweling squares), a cot, blankets, a pram, a dolly highchair, empty nappy cream containers and a pretend changing mat.

Doctor's kit

An old bag filled with clothes pegs for injections, bandages, empty ointment containers and a stethoscope.

Wooden blocks

Make wooden blocks of all sizes from fallen branches. Children love to sand and beeswax or oil wood, ready for the play basket. Large planks of wood are great for inside and outside play. Tree stumps are fun to balance on.

Farmyard

Wooden animals, farm buildings and fences, coloured play cloths (old bits of material) for grass, ponds and fields.

Dolls' house and furniture

These can often be found in secondhand shops, or you can make them at home. Simple little dolls can also be made for the house.

Toys with wheels (that move!)

A wooden trolley, a big-wheeled lorry, cars, trucks, a train set. Pull-along toys, a hobby horse. Toddlers love to pull a toy on string; it helps them feel powerful!

Simple surprises

A wind-up music box, a jack-in-a-box, simple musical instruments.

Small table and chairs

A small table is great for a tea party. Turn it upside down and it becomes a boat! Add an old rope to tie it to the dock!

Large play

Simple wooden frames with shelves (Steiner-Waldorf play stands) for versatile creative play. These can be used to make cubbies, shops, kitchens and much more. Your sofa and cushions will make boats and tractors! Cardboard-box creations are always fun, including castles, dolls' houses, boats and a train.

Household equipment

Save old computers and keyboards, phones, headphones, briefcases, files, notepads, weighing scales and bags – these are perfect for play offices, post offices and shops.

For cubby building

Throw cotton bedspreads or large sheets over the dining-room table, add some cushions and a snack and you have a young child's haven and heaven. Make a teepee in the garden with bamboo poles, securing a big sheet around the frame with clothes pegs.

A basket of smaller cloths

Keep small cloths as they are very useful for tea parties and make-believe storytelling (they can represent oceans and green grass).

Housework

A low washing line, a little washing basket and clothes pegs, a small ironing board and pretend iron, a little broom, dustpan and brush all allow housework to include children's play.

Bathtime play

Create happiness in the bath with wooden boats, little pots and pans, old containers, seashells and spoons, funnels and sieves, dolls' clothes and a dolly to wash.

Outside Play

Daily outdoor adventures are important.

A sandpit with old baking equipment (pattie tins, sieves, pots and pans!) is a wonderful gift for children.

Add to the garden a cubby, planks of wood and tree stumps (to balance on); a little vegetable garden to plant magic seeds (and a little watering can and shovel); and a bug catcher for nature's wonders.

A little bike or trike gives many, many satisfied hours.

Bamboo garden poles tied together to make a teepee (cover with a big blanket or throw rug) create a magical space.

Put a smile on a child's face (and on the footpaths!) with large chalks for drawing.

Can there be a dirt pit, for mud pies?

Use what you find in nature to create a fairy garden.

Do some woodwork on a big log – use a pot of nails and a hammer (bang away under supervision) and perhaps an old toolbox and tools.

Paint the house with old paintbrushes and water.

Do you like camping? Children love having the tent put up inside to sleep in, or outside on a sunny day!

A swing set, or a tree branch with a hanging tyre, are wonderful additions.

Real Life Roles to Play

On local outings notice the real-life roles that might happily become imaginative and imitative play back at home. Hold young children up high at the post office or bank so they can see and interact. Staff often like a chat with little ones! Save objects that can be props for playing real-life roles:

Postperson or office worker – use old envelopes, an old bag or satchel, cut slots in cardboard boxes to use them as letterboxes (placed inside or outside), a bike to do the deliveries, stamps, an ink pad and rubber stamps, an old computer keyboard, pigeonholes or an accordian file, old phones, notepads and pens.

Tram or bus driver – use the sofa and pillows, old tickets and a hat.

Café cook and waiting staff – use all your play kitchen equipment, an apron, a pen and pad (for waiting on tables).

Fish and chip shop staff – use newspaper to wrap up shells and gum nuts.

Doctors and nurses – use simple hats and jackets, a bag or fishing-tackle box, old ointment containers, pegs for injections, bandages, and teddy – a willing patient!

Pilot – use old headphones, a captain's hat, a makeshift furniture airplane.

Train driver – use carriage chairs and boxes – remember to toot!

Tradespeople – use a toolbox with small old tools, a belt to hang things on.

Children do not need to play with toys from a toyshop,

especially the bright, plastic, battery-powered ones. There are endless opportunities for play, every day, in simple ways.

Reflection

Children are great imitators, so give them something great to copy!

The Importance of a Doll

A good doll teaches children about love and tenderness. A lovely doll will naturally encourage a child to care for it. Children will dress, feed (even breastfeed!), wrap, carry and push their beloved dolls in a pram. Through their tenderness to a doll, younger children will develop the capacity to love and care for another individual.

Joan Salter, in her wonderful book, *The Incarnating Child* (Hawthorn Press), explains:

> The little boy or girl who loves a special doll, caring for it tenderly, singing a lullaby as it is put to bed, is the adult who will be the loving, caring parent, nurse, doctor or welfare worker.

A doll is a special friend. Dolls made from natural materials make wonderful pals! A simply-formed, soft doll is easy to carry around, and chew! As children grow, they may choose a more formed doll. When they are still older, they can dress and plait hair on a doll themselves. The simple shape and features of soft, natural-fibre dolls allow increased imaginative play. In a child's hands, the soft, warm fabrics speak of goodness.

If you are thinking of buying a baby plastic doll, perhaps look first in a secondhand shop, or might you inherit a pre-loved one from a niece or nephew?

Teaching tenderness

Remember, dolls are for boys as well as girls, and they are especially important if there is a new baby brother or sister.

Environmental Issues

When deciding on appropriate toys, consider the environment too. What is the toy made from? Does it include toxins? Will it last or break? What will happen to it after its use – will it biodegrade in the ground or add to landfill?

Wooden and fabric toys are wonderful options; of course,

check that the wood source is plantation and ethical, and that there are no lead paints. Wooden toys hold the quality of warm wood in our children's hands. They are often simpler than toys made from other materials, like plastic, and this means they offer greater scope for imaginative play. They tend to last and last, and can be handed down from one generation to the next.

Plastic toys tend to break very quickly. Plastic is made from oil (petroleum), and it is hard to dispose of in a sustainable way. If you are buying plastic toys, buy from secondhand shops and pass them on. If you can find a wooden alternative, then so much the better.

The Play Area

The way toys are set up and made accessible to children has a profound effect on the quality of play. Especially in the earlier years, children prefer to play when we're about. They like to be alongside an adult: 'Look at me!' This may mean your busy home spaces will be a little messy for a while, but play and heartfelt connections are made.

It is common to see toys in children's bedrooms or in a family room or play room. Children are expected to play in isolation, away from the heart of the action and centre of the home. Where do families spend their time? A kitchen and dining room combined is usually the room in most continual use. Can you create a play corner here? Perhaps add a bookshelf with toys to your lounge? When we shower, a basket of toys nearby in the bedroom is lovely. Try different areas to see what works best in your home. A play kitchen near the real kitchen is handy and inspiring! There is something quite wonderful about cooking, or sitting, near a child who is happily playing.

The way toys are stored can also help to foster creative play, and this requires thought. Avoid a toy box with a shutting lid. If we cannot see them, the child will not see them either. Being thrown on top of one another is somewhat disrespectful to beloved toys. Ideally, display toys on shelves in a play corner or on a wall using bookcases and open baskets. This allows the child to see where they are, and it is a loving place where they live after tidy-up time.

Something to Try

Take a minute, close your eyes, and imagine the play corner, toys and your outside play space from your child's perspective. Is there some way to make it more nourishing and magical? Look to the toy list in this chapter for inspiration.

Dusty Gnome Cleans our Home

If something has to stay up for more play the next day, put a cloth over it. Otherwise, leave the shelves and play area tidy after playtime or at the end of each day. This shows children the benefits of being organised, tidy and respectful. A really untidy house and play corner can add to unsettled, disruptive and even bored feelings in children. There are creative ways of tidying up; it does not need to be a grind. Try singing a little song together:

There was a little dusty gnome,
He said, 'It's time to clean our home!'
Round, round, round,
Swish, swish, swish,
Clean our home.

Tidy up with children, working together as a family. Have a special tidy-up basket for the toy animals. Have a special pack-away trolley or big truck to wheel things back home. Lovingly tuck a doll back in bed, saying, 'There you go, goodnight!' By doing this we are showing respect and love for the toys. Pack-away time can be playing too: 'Help! I am all alone and lost!' calls a toy pig, left on the floor. Can we pack everything away together before the timer goes 'Ping?' Role-model tidying, and creatively encourage children to help. Now the house is tidy, it's time for a bath, story or tea!

Messy, Big Play – A Great Way!

Great play experiences can also be really big, and it's fine to take over a space for a while. Whatever a young child has experienced in life, be it a tram or bus ride, a hospital visit, the post office, the supermarket, they love to act it all out again – and again! They need time and space for this. It is a necessary and joyful play experience for them, to process and understand the world they live in. This is sacred play – only children can do it. For them, it is real; their imagination makes it so. A wooden block is a packet of butter on a supermarket shelf, large shells and gum nuts wrapped in newspaper are fish and chips!

This wonderful big play may require our help to set up: a row of chairs and a plank become a train (remember those used tickets!); the sofa is transformed into a big bus; a few items from the cupboard set up on shelves are the supermarket. When you are all at a loose end, throw a big sheet or cotton bed spread over the dining room table, plus a few cushions and a blanket underneath, and we have an exciting new home for afternoon tea and play.

Often children play with household items, so for a while we may need to live without them! My laundry basket was always the funnel for the steam train, with an up-turned little table and chairs as carriages. Balancing on planks and tree stumps during big play is great for children's coordination and sense of fun and achievement. Is there someone in your house who loves to climb on things? Set up big challenging play, including an outside climbing frame.

The Rhythmical Quality of Play

Children's play often has a rhythmical quality to it: a child plays one thing for a while, and then changes. They may like to keep their homemade bus set up for three or four days. Children play with one scenario for a while, experiencing it deeply, and then they move on. Keep unused toys, as children may surprise us by revisiting them again later, with renewed gusto, even in a year or so. When my boy was turning ten, he still got the felt animals and play cloths out from time to time to build an elaborate farm with his younger sister.

Sandpit magic

The Sandpit and Dirty Play Outside

The imaginative play that can happen in a sandpit is wonderful – every home with children benefits from a sandpit in the garden! Include some old kitchen equipment and away they go!

Sandpits can be constructed using big logs sometimes found on the side of the road: make a log circle, line the inside with plastic, and phone the local building suppliers for sand (mention it is for a sandpit, as builders' sand can be a little coarse). Or use an old paddling pool filled with sand.

So your sandpit does not become a litter tray for cats, cover it with a big plastic sheet when it's not in use.

Fed up with finding sand inside? When coming in, sing a little song at the door while brushing off clothes and stamping feet. Encourage everyone to take their shoes off and tap them together.

Children's play, particularly outside, means getting dirty – often! Dirty clothes are the sign of a good day's playing.

Secondhand clothing eliminates the preciousness that comes with new clothes. They also mean reduced costs for you and the planet. Is there a family member or a friend who can pass on clothes?

Toys on the Go

Play can go everywhere: take a little purse or bag to the shops, bring teddy on a car journey, carry a little backpack with special things to a café, push a doll's pram to the park. Before heading out, consider how children can still iMagine, iMitate and have an iMpulse to move wherever you are going. Children will be happier with play toys joining the journey, even though parents may end up pushing the doll's pram back up the hill!

The Adult's Role when a Child Plays

What is the ideal role for a parent while children are playing? You don't need to take on the role of entertainer to foster a positive play experience. Adults who continually read stories, do puzzles and play games can make the child reliant on them to play, and after a while this drives parents crazy. Sometimes it is helpful to start a child off playing, by setting up a play scene or space (a farm on the floor, a cubby under the dining-room table) and gently remove ourselves, working or sitting nearby. Occasionally, ask for something from the 'café' or buy something in the 'shop', to keep the play flowing, but we are not our child's exclusive play-friend. The imaginative world is theirs, not ours.

An adult cannot venture into the world of imagination for long periods in the same way a child does. It is false: imaginative play is a child's truth, not an adult's. Be busy with other things – perhaps reading, housework, or a creative project – while your child is playing nearby. This nurtures independence in the child's play. Our awareness can be continually with our child, sharing little conversations and stepping in where necessary, while fostering independent play. A happy playing child means a happy parent! A parent who has time for themselves while a child is playing is more fulfilled. Try it and see!

Play may be for short times before we connect together to eat, to cuddle or to share a story. Do not expect a young child to necessarily play for long periods without us – although sometimes they will! I have found that if I focus on my children first (set them up to play, stop to read a story, include them in my work or cuddle them when they need it), I will then have time for myself while they play. Trying to get things done when they are unsettled is a recipe for tears.

In *The Vital Role of Play in Early Childhood* (WECAN), Joan Almon says:

> My experience is that children thrive when given space for indoor and outdoor play and have a sense of comfort from knowing that a caring adult is nearby, preferably doing things like gardening, woodwork, cooking or cleaning.

Stages of Play

At the age of four or five, a child may turn to their sibling or friend and say, 'Let's play boats', and they make a game up together. Before this time, they will most often play by themselves or alongside another (parallel play). At this young age, play can be short and close to you.

If a baby or toddler is present, protect an older child's play from being knocked down, allowing it to be sacred and special. Set up their play while baby is asleep, or create a special area, blocked away from the toddler. Perhaps put a toddler gate on the older child's door to give them protected space in their own room.

Non-stereotyped Play

While it is true that my daughter plays with dolls more than her brother, they both play with most toys together. Let us encourage the development of well-balanced men and women. Boys also like to play at cooking in the sandpit, cafés, doctors and nurses and more. Let us educate our boys to cook, clean and wash, as these are skills they will need. My daughter loves playing with toy cars, and no doubt she will need to check the oil in adult life. And perhaps to plan the road system! My recommended toy list is for both sexes: offer children all choices and see what happens.

It is interesting to observe what inspires an individual child. My firstborn loved play cooking; he got great benefit from a play café, with bowls and shells, and little pads to take orders. He rocked away on his rocking horse and never tired of his game of doctors' surgery. My younger had a fetish for beads and handbags; she never went near the rocking horse and turned the café into a dog's world when she inherited the play space. She also plays with toy cars more than her brother. Be open to what children are drawn to. Which play experiences nourish them?

Children who experience good play opportunities are more settled, relaxed, balanced and happy. Play experiences improve a child's mood and behaviour. Create wonderful spaces, provide imaginative toys and allow time for play in homes. Remember the real three 'i' words of childhood: iMagination, iMitation, and the iMpulse to move. Children reap the rewards, now and later, in childhood and adult life.

A Word from a Dad – Michael

A dad's body is a toy, a climbing frame, a helicopter, a horse, a tunnel and many other things. I was the Whizzer King to my daughter and her friends. 'Hold on and I will spin you around!'

A Word from Seven-year-old Jayson

My sister and I play doctors and farms together. She puts all the animals in fields while I use my big truck to move fences around. The fences are bits of wood.

Real Life Story
Melissa – Dolls

A few years ago my daughters, who were then aged five and seven, and I read the story 'Little House in the Big Woods'. The real-life heroine, Laura Ingalls Wilder, had nothing more than a corn cob wrapped in a handkerchief for a doll baby. The baby's name was Susan, and she was a good doll. Laura loved that doll, even though she didn't have an expensive porcelain face, golden curls or a lace dress. In its simplicity, that wrapped corn cob allowed a little girl to explore her own emotional life: to nurture, to tell her deepest thoughts, to scold, to cradle. It allowed her to imagine what her doll looked like and who her doll was, for herself.

A child's doll, if we really ponder it, represents themselves. The more that is left to their own imaginations, the more they will be free to discover themselves through play. So, after reading 'Little House in the Big Woods', I was delighted to find my daughters had raided the fridge for corn, found themselves a pillowslip each, and made their own corn cob dolls. They immersed themselves in their roles as mothers, and you would have thought those little corn cobs were real babies, they were treated with such dedication!

My daughters have had a few other dolls before and since, even a few Barbies that well-meaning friends felt they simply must have. The Barbies got a big 'ooh' and 'aah' the first day and were played with intensely for a week, but have never come out of the cupboard since! By far my girls' favourite dolls were the simple ones that were made from cloth, by hand. They have small dolls for their dolls' house, and they each have one large doll, with the same hair and eye colour as themselves. These dolls became favourite friends and confidants.

The big dolls have been on family holidays, car trips and often sat at the dinner table with us. The smaller dolls act out innumerable stories – even now, aged eight and ten, my daughters are still playing with their dolls' house. Sometimes, when I have a moment, I stop and listen to their play at the door – and I am always astounded at the complexities of their young lives, which I hear coming through their play! I hear the stories of bullying at school, of friendships formed, of sisters fighting and loving each other, of what Daddy said to the silly driver on the road, and, yes, often I hear myself mirrored there – sometimes I like what I hear – other times I wince! I hear two children learning about all the wonderful shades of what it is to be human, through play and imagination, and I am so very, very glad that those dolls have a more interesting life than wearing high heels and miniskirts!

Checklist – Play

1. Remember, imagination is more important than knowledge; choose toys that aid imaginative play.

2. How can you set up space inside and outside so children can move?

3. Go through the list of recommended toys in this chapter before your child's next birthday or Christmas. Happy secondhand shopping!

4. Invite children to do household chores with you in a fun way. Adult work is child's play!

5. Never throw a cardboard box away!

6. Set up play areas in rooms where the family spends time together in the day; display toys on shelves and in open baskets.

7. Tidy-up time can be fun!

8. Help to set up play, then stand back! Maybe intervene to keep a flow. Avoid being the entertainer, fearing they may – perish the thought – be bored!

9. Reflect: what sort of toys and play does your unique child like?

10. Remember to seek out quality toys (not cheap quantity toys that end up in landfill).

11. Buy secondhand plastic toys and pass them on when you're finished with them, or, better, use wooden alternatives.

12. Collect items for play from secondhand shops: they are kind to the wallet, the environment and children's imagination.

13. Collect natural objects for play and wonder.

14. Does your child have a special dolly friend?

15. Find a friend, relative or neighbour who can pass down children's clothes. Can you also hand on your children's clothes to another household?

16. Buy clothes that can withstand getting dirty; a couple of 'best' outfits is enough.

Chapter Seven
What's Stopping Play Today?

Play is the work of the child.

MARIA MONTESSORI

Today's society has highly stimulating toys, TV and electronic games, and a fast-paced lifestyle. Nurturing a child's imaginative play requires understanding from parents. In addition, there is pressure to teach the young child with so-called educational toys, and to fill up time with outside activities and long periods away from the home environment. Fast life, fast learning and highly stimulating, commercial toys and electronic games create a negative effect on the child's natural tendency to play.

Highly Stimulating Toys

The more a toy does for a child, the less they have to do themselves. If a machine requires children to push buttons to care for a dog or to dress a doll, their finger muscles get developed, but that is it. When children dress dolly, wrapping her in a blanket to sleep, talking to her, pushing her in a pram, it is quite, quite different. If a toy train moves around a track while flashing and making puffing noises, what is there for children to do? Just watch! Compare this to the child who creates the track, pushes the train around by hand, and makes train sounds: 'choof, choof!' What happens to this latter child's imagination? It grows! When considering stimulating toys, less is definitely more.

The Kindergarten Experiment

At teacher's college, I learnt of an early-childhood play experiment. Researchers left a toy that spun around, flashed and made noises in a room and then observed children's interactions with the toy. The children explored the toy for a while but once they seemed to have it all worked out, they left it alone. These researchers also observed children engaged with a long pole that had a triangle shape at the top left in the same room. This object became, variously, a flag on a castle, a walking stick, a sail on a boat. It was played with for a greater time than the whiz-bang (unimaginative) toy. This wooden pole could come alive with the children's energy; it could be transformed with their imagination, be part of their own creativity. This adaptable toy was healthy for children.

I use the word 'healthy' because when children imaginatively play, they become alive and bright in the moment. Play stimulates the brain and the body moves naturally in the way it wants to. Children who are heavily exposed to overstimulating toys may in fact become lazy, wanting the world to entertain them. Tantrums increase, as addiction to being stimulated sets in.

The importance of child's play is reinforced by Rahima Baldwin Dancy in *You are Your Child's First Teacher* (Celestial Arts):

> Just as it is important not to skip steps like crawling in
> physical development, so the age of fantasy should be
> honoured as a valuable part of normal development.

Sound Waves

Children are often bombarded by noise nowadays (as are adults too): a constant background of TV sound, radio, noisy toys, audio books, music, movies and electronic games, at home and in the car. When, during the day, can children have periods of quietness, time for imaginative play, time to communicate with loved ones?

What happens when children are constantly stimulated and entertained through their sight and sound senses? Their nervous systems are continuously stimulated! They may demand that the world entertain them. Because of annoying background sound, the adults around are made increasingly grumpy too!

Interestingly, as a teacher, I have noticed changes in children's behaviour during the past twenty years. In many classrooms now, there are children who find it hard to sit still, in silence, working. They tap, hum, drum on the table, sway on their chair, oblivious to their own noises.

The importance of play

The Question of Television

There are many discussions in the media on the subject of TV and electronic games. The World Health Organisation (WHO) recommends no television for children under two years of age. Prolonged early television watching has been linked to early language disorders – social interaction and speech development are missed because children are sitting passively in front of screens.

Martin Large explains the benefits of reduced TV in *Set Free Childhood* (Hawthorn Press):

> Children will talk more, play longer, be less demanding for junk foods, know how to occupy themselves, do their household chores, sleep better and be more geared up to learning skills.

I have found that in early childhood it can be easier to give television a total miss. What children do not know, they do not ask for. If you then decide to introduce television, be conscious of when (and why) it is introduced. Is a pattern or expectation being set up for the child? A regular rhythm can help with expectations, 'Friday night is home-movie night. Get out the popcorn!' Our rule, once we introduced TV, was never in the morning or daytime and only on weekend nights. My children are now older and, apart from weekend evenings, we select certain programmes and enjoy them together as a family. The TV still never goes on in the daytime. If the sun's up, there's a life to be lived! Make how and when you introduce TV your choice.

If you decide to introduce some screen time, it can be wonderful to choose the home-movies you have filmed yourself for this special occasion. Children usually love to watch themselves: for years my children preferred their home-movies to any commercial films or TV.

Be aware that most children's movies seem to have a 'baddie' element, which can frighten children and create unnecessary nightmares and fears. Watching a scene (complete with graphic colour, movement and sound) is quite different to listening to a story and creating images yourself. The images and characters experienced can powerfully replay, especially at night time, when children feel particularly vulnerable. Children can become mesmerised and, even though the scenes frighten them, they do not turn away. Watch movies together, make it a social event and observe children's responses; you may have to turn off! Always adhere to movie age ratings; they are there for a reason – to protect children's brains. Nevertheless, many movies assessed as acceptable for children are scary.

If children watch a particular movie repetitively, they may become obsessed and think about the characters all the time. This may take the child out of the present moment. The images often replay in their mind and take over their play. Does this movie or programme include images of kindness, wonder and joy, a love of life?

Many children's television programmes include commercial advertisements, which influence children to become demanding consumers. Numerous products will be branded with your child's favourite TV programme characters and logos in mass commercial merchandising. I have my favourite TV programmes, but how would I feel with the image on my bed cover, drink bottle, t-shirt and even underpants. Could my brain think of anything else?

Turned off Emotionally

Can you catch up on news on the internet or TV or in a newspaper once your child is in bed?

There is so much hardship and sorrow in the news. This can be flashed before our eyes, followed by a happy advertisement or weather report! We get close and personal with terror and suffering, but often feel nothing, numbed to the experience by the screen and the time of day. How does this affect our children? Does it numb them emotionally too?

Be conscious that if we turn on the TV, this starts a potential new pattern for the child. Create clear rhythms that you are happy with and can stick to. Remember that viewing habits are laid down early, so decide how much TV is to be in your children's lives.

British children who spend most time in front of televisions and computer screens have lower self-esteem and greater emotional problems, according to a study published by Public Health England. The results were reported in the Independent on August 28, 2013, and Professor Kevin Fenton of Public

Health England was quoted as saying, "The greater the time spent in front of the screen, the greater the negative impact on both behavioural and emotional issues relating to the child's development." Electronic games have a similar effect and are highly stimulating and addictive.

If children keep asking to watch the TV, explain gently in words that they can understand, 'Too much television is bad for your beautiful growing brain; let's play, cook, go for a walk, read a story instead!' or 'I want to talk to you while we cook, let's be together.'

Be a role model for your children: turn off during family time and keep meal times sacred (no electronic devices).

Something to Try

Trying to decrease TV time or electronic games? Cover the TV with a coloured cloth and place electronic gadgets up high when not in use. Out of sight, out of mind! Make a chart or, for younger children, a photo album of all the play choices at home: drawing, Lego, dolly play, cars, time outside in the garden, train set, books… If children ask to watch TV, get the play photos book or chart and explain, 'Your body likes to move and your brain to imagine,' and ask them to choose something else to do.

If my children ever say they are bored, I tell them: 'There is no such thing with a creative mind!'

The Real World – What is it?

Some people comment that children need to 'live in the real world', meaning the modern world of TV programmes and electronic games! This is a funny comment when looked at closely: the 'real world' is not the TV, computer games and hand-held entertainers; it is, in fact, the life that children are missing, that which is going on around them now, here!

Would we sit a dog in front of a movie of a walk, and then say, 'Great, the dog has been walked'? No! Think of children sitting in front of hours of cooking, dancing and play on TV screens or electronic games. Have they experienced these activities? They have not; it is not the real world.

The 'real' world also extends to the look of toys: 'real' is not a large-breasted doll with unrealistically long legs, it is a doll that resembles the true human body. It is not a grotesque robot but a cow or sheep on a play farm. Real toys hold the magic of life, of animals and our daily human tasks. When buying toys ask, 'Does this toy resemble the real world around my child?' and 'Does it teach them about real life on Earth?'

Dad is the best play thing!

Boys' Toys: What Do They Encourage?

What about gender-based toys? If we go down the boys' toy aisle in major shops and department stores, we're met with images of violence, gruesomeness and speed. Do we really want all of these qualities in our boys' play? What type of play and thoughts do these toys encourage? A child will imitate.

Boys (especially) need rough-and-tumble play, with a human. They can also develop testosterone by digging a deep hole, or kicking a goal. Boys enjoy toy diggers and paper aeroplanes and pretend cooking – there are many famous male chefs! Toys do not have to be extreme in 'action' and grotesqueness.

At a parenting talk, a kindergarten teacher talked about toy guns as having a powerful allure for boys. She said even if you ban everything that resembles a gun you'll find boys may use their penises in the bath as toy guns because they are so driven to play this game. If this is the case with your children, perhaps consider gun toy replacements (sticks or a pretend bow and arrow). Teach children to point at trees or cans, never at animals or people. This is usually a stage and lasts a short time. Avoid threatening or scaring anyone. Play firemen and point your hose instead! In the hot days of summer fill washing-up bottles with water, for a game of squirt fun!

On a similar note, I find buying boys' pyjamas difficult: they have images of speed, skulls and dinosaurs, not soothing pictures for sleep. If you find some with relaxing patterns, buy sizes up for the next few years!

Clothes and Toys 'For Girls'

Protect the purity and dreaminess of children. Reject clothing styles that aim at fashion consciousness or sexiness. Children need comfortable, warm, easy-play, easy-wash clothes.

I carefully avoid saying, 'That looks pretty,' or 'You look cute,' in relation to girls' clothes. There is no need to make children aware or conscious of dressing a certain way. Let children be free from image; a child's smiling face is the most wonderful thing, not their clothing. This caution also applies to choosing toys: young girls can be influenced by the clothes a doll wears too.

The girls' toy aisle is full of flawless, full-bodied, plastic, large-breasted images of women, or girls with large heads and full make-up, dyed hair and fashion clothes. Do such toys fill children with an unrealistic and unattainable ideal of a woman's body shape? Are they also a slippery slide into the shallow world of appearances, of fashion consciousness for the young? Here I go on my bandwagon! As the Dalai Lama likes to say, what do you think?

I actually do remember getting my first doll of this kind at eight years or so; I remember looking at it for a while, then deciding that I was quite an unattractive child. If your children play with these dolls, be creative and make clothes together, or find knitted ones in charity shops. Occasionally point out the artificiality of the dolls. Perhaps comment, nonchalantly, 'Whose body is actually like that, such long legs and big breasts!' 'No one really looks like this: how tiny is her waist and long her legs? She has been stretched!'

Can you imagine a little girl pretending to breastfeed a Barbie doll? When I suggest this, most people say 'Yuk!' Why? Because it is a doll suitable for fashion, not nurturing.

Sometimes relatives and friends choose presents that we wouldn't. What to do? A quiet word about what may be a suitable new toy might help, or a suggestion about good shops or websites to look at. I do feel it's important to politely receive all toys. My assumption is that those who give have kind intent: they want to make us happy, so, a happy 'thank you' for the gift of giving is required. The child plays for a while with the new toys, the novelty wears off, and the top shelf of the cupboard is a good place: out of sight, out of mind. They can be taken quietly to the secondhand shop perhaps, or stay up there for a rainy day.

Facts, Facts and More Dry Facts - Yawn!

Toy and electronic game companies are never going to publicise the very useful knowledge that children learn colours, shapes and numbers from real life conversations and imaginative play. I find that children naturally absorb knowledge when they are introduced to it during play and everyday life. 'Look, that brown dog is jumping over the tall fence.' Imaginative play makes children intelligent! In *The Vital Role of Play in Early Childhood* (WECAN), Joan Almond reinforces this finding:

> Research in Germany in the 1970s showed that by fourth grade children who had attended play-orientated kindergartens surpassed those from academic-orientated kindergartens in physical, social, emotional and mental development.

Albert Einstein himself said,

> Imagination is more important than knowledge. For knowledge is limited to all we know and understand, while imagination embraces the entire world and all there ever will be to know and understand.

No toys with academic content or TV programmes or games are required to educate our young children, just imaginative play.

I am not against technology: I love my iPhone, particularly face-timing my relatives many miles away. However, I understand that technology will wait for my children, it has a place after their imagination has been used up!

Reflection

I saw a cartoon of a child sitting alone in front of a TV screen. The caption read, 'Danger! Child not at play!'

A Word from Seven-year-old Jayson

Yesterday the baby played with a roll of cardboard. My sister used to play with an empty milk carton on the floor in the kitchen. I had a three-stringed guitar and a rocking horse, which I liked a lot. I liked to hide under the stairs!

Real Life Story
Stuart – Turning off the TV

My children have never been allowed to watch unlimited TV, and morning viewing was definitely out. I warned them for months that if the television went on in the morning, I would take the TV away. Being normal kids they pushed the boundaries time and time again. Our eldest (seventeen years), was adamant he would watch his half-hour show each morning. We relented and agreed, as long as the twins (eight years) were not in viewing range.

Inadvertently the twins ended up in front of the screen, and the half-hour show would become two half-hour shows. Morning duties were haphazard, if done at all. There was continual stress about the children being ready for school.

One morning I yet again insisted that I did not want the younger children exposed to TV in the morning and that if it was not turned off immediately I would take it away.

Truth be known, the thought of no TV was an unpleasant thought for me, which is why the situation dragged on for so long. If I took the TV away, what would I do when I needed to veg out in the evenings?

This time, I bit the bullet and packed up the TV for a while. The children watched open-mouthed in dismay. But two minutes later, my eldest was doing his homework, one twin was sweeping the floor and the other was reading a book. That evening I played the guitar with my oldest son. Sanity had returned to our home.

Checklist – Play – What's stopping us?

1. Look for toys that resemble the real world (fairies included!).

2. Set limits to screen time for children, and choose programmes and DVDs wisely (home movies you have taken yourself are a lovely way to go).

3. Redirect a child to play using a photo album or chart.

4. Include great play spaces, shared tasks, stories, outings and craft with children, then limited screen time will not leave such a hole, and connection will flourish.

5. When buying a toy, consider: how does it create opportunities for imagination and wonder?

6. Beware of boys' toys that overemphasise violence, extreme speed and gruesomeness. What is the toy saying to and encouraging in children?

7. Is there enough time at your home for play?

8. Do your children see lots of things worth imitating: home activities, community and nature outings?

9. Place unwanted toys in the cupboard for a rainy day.

10. Praise children's beautiful smiling faces, not their clothes!

Chapter Eight

The Twelve Senses and the Seven Life Processes

Touch has a memory.

JOHN KEATS

The Twelve Senses

Rudolf Steiner talks of a human being having twelve senses, not just the five most people know (sight, smell, taste, sound and touch). Babies and young children sense things completely. An infant's whole body takes in every impression. In *The Developing Child: The First Seven Years* (WECAN), Lisa Gromicko says:

> The infant and the young child are totally given over to the environment, extending themselves into it, and actually consuming every single detail of life that meets the senses. Every color, smell, sound, taste, texture, word, shape, activity, and even the moods of others – everything is taken in.

What are the Twelve Senses Steiner identifies, and how can we make sure they are nurtured for a well-balanced, calm, healthy childhood?

The Sense of Touch

Touch speaks a thousand words: love, safety, trust, connection and comfort. Human touch has the power to create settled and healthy young children.

Carla Hannaford says in *Smart Moves: Why learning is not all in your head* (Great Ocean Publishers):

> Touch right after birth stimulates growth of the body's sensory nerve endings involved in motor movements, spatial orientation and visual perception.

Touch speaks a thousand words

Joseph Chilton Pearce pioneered the 'Kangaroo Project', in which premature babies are carried around in a sling (pouch!), next to the mother's skin. Babies with this ongoing skin-to-skin contact grew at a faster rate.

Touch increases the happy hormone, oxytocin. When a young child wants to hold your hand, to sit on your lap ('I would like to feel cocooned by you') or join you in the bath, it is a special time. Remember to slow down and enjoy these special touch moments throughout the day. Be creative: touch can also mean 'butterfly kisses' (using the eye lashes to tickle), tummy rubs, head massages at bedtime, chase and tickle games and cuddling.

Every child has a different experience of touch. Find your child's soft spot. One child may love kisses, while another finds them wet and soggy. Yuk! Some children may love their head being rubbed, others their tummy. What does your child like?

The gift of being lovingly touched when younger leads to comfortable feelings around touch when older. Start early: enrol in a baby massage course, or follow ideas from a book or your own intuition. Later, during the toddler and childhood years, remember to use the power of touch to provide a child with feelings of safety and warmth, and to settle a child's behaviour. Make touch a common occurrence every day; it is a precious gift indeed.

The Sense of Life

The sense of life is the inner sense that allows us to understand our own constitution, to know whether we feel well or not and to monitor our emotional well-being. Through this sense we understand how we feel at any given time. For a younger child, the sense of life is: 'Am I physically and emotionally comfortable?'

Babies and young children cry because their sense of life has been disturbed. This distress may be caused by physical hunger, being over-tired or over-stimulated, too warm, too cold, needing a nappy change or feeling a sense of separation from a loved one. It is important to respond immediately. The first part of the baby's brain to develop is the brain stem, or reptilian brain. This rapid development occurs from the third trimester of pregnancy to fifteen months of age. The work of the brain stem is self-preservation: monitoring the outer world (through sensory input) and activating the body to respond. At a young age, crying is the main form of communication. When babies' cries are responded to quickly and not allowed to escalate, they are much easier to settle.

A child's sense of life is positively stimulated by what we discuss in this book: a slow and loving home rhythm, where there are periods to truly connect and bond; daily mealtime and bedtime rhythms that bring beauty and magic, regular food and rest periods that nurture a child's sense of life; healthy and imaginative play options, which create rosy cheeks; using the hands to create and feel competent; healing stories which speak to the heart; feeling connected to the earth and a growing respect for nature with her many treasures; creative discipline that helps a child feel understood and avoids the fear of reprimands and other unsafe emotional feelings. (See also my book, *Turning Tears into Laughter: Creative Discipline for the Toddler and Preschool Years.*)

Be aware of your child's sense of life, how they are feeling in any given moment, and, where required, provide positive 'connected' rhythms, a new play experience, a restful space, or a healing story.

It is good for us to be aware of our own sense of life. We, too, can override this in our fast-paced existence. Imbalance leads to illness (and higher stress levels). Parents who attend my workshops exclaim, 'This is for me, too, not just for my children! I am learning to live a more balanced life.' Be aware of the breath! A happy parent influences a child's sense of life.

When babies cry, or children are over-emotional, ask, 'What is affecting their sense of life? How can I help?'

The Sense of Movement

Early movement patterns are wonderful to observe: how babies go from rolling and wriggling to crawling, to sitting, to walking. All the stages are important in the development of a child's sense of movement. If these movement patterns are stilted, especially crawling, a visit to an osteopath may be worthwhile.

Once on their feet, let children explore, run and climb on a daily basis; movement patterns are good for brain neurons. I teach a 'Movement and Learning' programme to children. I have seen the correlation between difficulty coordinating the body, and academic and emotional challenges. Nimble body movements create nimble minds! Provide time in the garden or park for climbing trees, swinging, balancing on walls and climbing up and down stairs and steps (assist at first, role-model how to move safely). When children are older, encourage hopscotch, skipping and other gross-motor childhood games. Fun in indoor and outdoor movement is paramount for a healthy childhood. More is going on than meets the eye – movement creates healthy brains and bodies! In the Christmas stocking each year, include a movement game (a skipping rope, large chalk for hopscotch, or a balancing game).

Today's world restricts movements: computer games require a fixed stare and finger movements only! Young children's bodies are primed to move for most of the day.

The Sense of Balance

The ear has three semi-circular tubes or canals. This formation allows us to have a relationship with three-dimensional space, with objects above and below us, to the right and left, behind and infront of us. Balance develops with movement. Babies have a drive to try over and over again: to roll over, crawl, sit up, stand, and walk. It is important that a child achieves these milestones unassisted: this develops muscles, as well as pleasing the will to accomplish. Avoid baby walkers, or propping up a baby in a sitting position.

A baby's sense of balance improves when they are carried in slings, and with the use of baby hammocks, rocking chairs, with rides in the pram, and with bouncing on the knee to nursery rhymes. Later there are wonderful balancing adventures in the garden and local park.

In *Movement, Gesture and Language in the Life of the Young Child* (WECAN), Bronja Zahlingen describes rocking motions while growing up:

And then there is rocking, first gently in the cradle, half dreaming with soft songs, like being carried along the waves of life's water. Then this motion becomes stronger when they are riding on the knee… When children are a bit older, the rocking motion is there in their swinging, which grows more courageous.

The sense of balance

Planks and tree stumps create balancing challenges in the back garden. While out walking, children love to balance on walls ('Hold my hand'). Swings and bikes are fun, and excellent for a child's sense of balance. Is there a tree to climb? Great! Try to avoid saying 'Be careful or you will fall!' Instead use positive reminders such as 'Hold on tight'. Shadow, if need be, with hands underneath the child's body. Remember that balancing movements and adventurous acts (with some guidance and support, maybe) stimulate the child's brain. Let's be balanced!

The Sense of Smell

The sense of smell is already highly developed in a baby. It is important to consider the smells that surround children: look for natural cleaning products and baby care goods with minimal or no artificial chemicals and perfumes. The mother's natural scent is the most wonderful scent to her baby, so avoid masking personal aromas. Beware of household cleaning items and room deodorisers, as the smells are often synthetic and include toxic chemicals.

Develop a child's sense of smell with the natural scent of home baking and fresh flowers on the table. When on a nature walk, smell the flowers together, and the grass after rain.

The Sense of Taste

To nurture a child's sense of taste, homemade baby foods are ideal. Continue with an additive-free childhood. Additives (colours, flavours, preservatives, flavour enhancers) can have an adverse effect on children's behaviour and mood swings. Fresh is best. Fresh foods stimulate taste buds, encourage lifelong healthy habits, and are kinder on our pockets and our Earth – fewer wrappers!

The benefits of fresh foods (biodynamic, organic and non-genetically modified when possible) include higher vitamin and mineral content, no additive side effects, and – wait for it – delicious taste! The point is simple: nurture children's sense of taste by eating real foods, creating homemade meals and sharing cooking skills from the minute they can hold a spoon. The kitchen is not for display; it is the heart of the home.

Real, fresh foods contain hidden secrets. A carrot slice looks like a human eye, and it is good for the eyes! Kidney beans are great for kidneys; a walnut resembles a brain, and is good for ours!

Taste bud preferences are laid down early; babies come with pristine bodies – let's keep them that way! A young child's taste buds are very sensitive to textures and tastes, and a child can suddenly change, from eating everything, to refusing to eat once-loved foods. There is a section in my book *Turning Tears into Laughter: Creative Discipline for the Toddler and Preschool Years* to deal with this, and, you may like to go back to the Happy Fruit and Vegetable Plate from Chapter One and a whiteboard checklist of food groups to encourage healthy eating habits.

The Sense of Sight

The simple things in life nurture a baby's sight, the most important being a loved one's smiling face. Look into your child's eyes and smile throughout the day! Lying under a tree, seeing light play through the leaves; watching an animal or bird; simple toys made from natural materials; everyday objects – all these develop the sense of sight, naturally and beautifully. Objects and toys do not have to be bright primary colours for a child to see them! Clothing and furnishings can be pastel for a baby, soothing for their sleep. A soft lilac or pink cloth over the bassinet or pram cocoons in a lovely hue.

Avoid heavily cluttered and messy areas; calmness comes with tidiness (and things can be found).

Natural objects and plenty of time in nature nurture natural eyesight. Children's eyes require natural flowing movements – encourage looking left and right, up and down, far away, and close up. All work the eye muscles beautifully. When in the garden and on local walks, point out the beautiful sights of flowers, animals and bugs. What can we see to nurture the eyes?

The Sense of Warmth

Babies sense the warmth or coolness of their bodies from birth; our bodies relax in warm temperatures, and contract in cold ones. Warmth is good for overall health. Wear cotton vests under clothes, and layer clothing. Dress children in a hat and socks and shoes when outside in the cooler months (thirty per cent of heat loss is from the top of the head). Wear a hat too, so you are a good role-model. Keep the body's focus on growing organs and not the survival mode of keeping warm. But don't overheat! Allow for individual difference.

At bedtime in the winter months, a hot-water bottle, as well as warm milk, is nurturing. Place a hot-water bottle towards the bottom of the bed too. It's hard to sleep with cold feet. Cuddles always provide bodily warmth. Remember that our soul warmth is important warmth. Love will warm the hearts of children.

The Sense of Hearing

By five months in the womb, the foetus responds to sounds. When babies are born, hearing is excellent. The best sound for babies and young children is a natural voice, particularly Mummy's and Daddy's. We tend to speak to babies in a high, singing voice; we instinctively know that this nurtures children. Listening to a lullaby or a little story is priceless for the ears! Loud noises, busy traffic, TV or radio, and frequent background recorded music and TV or electronic sounds are best kept to a minimum for us all.

A singing voice, rather than a talking voice, can be lovely for small children while completing daily tasks. After the bath, 'This is the way we dry our...' Children have a keen ear for a singing voice, and it soothes them.

Spaces of total quiet and peace, like resting places for sight, are required to truly nurture the sense of hearing. Walter Holtzapfel MD, author of *The Human Organs* (Floris Books), explains that increased prevalence of acoustics and optical stimuli not only attack the nervous system but also lead to changes in a child's circulation. Silence is a whole and wonderful sound (not a lonely sound as some may feel).

Extended times of quiet encourage imaginative play, communicating with others, and listening to the subtle sounds of life on Earth. They also create a more relaxed and settled child, happy to have peaceful silence. To feel peaceful we require a peaceful environment.

The Sense of Speech

Following on from the sense of hearing is the sense of speech. The young child requires natural voices, with clear, loving speech, to imitate. Speak and sing to young children throughout the day, so they are surrounded by the goodness of your speech. Young children love the sound of their own voices; nurture their speech with family communication, and by singing nursery rhymes and lullabies together. Avoid loud and harsh voices. Natural communicating, storytelling and singing (as outlined throughout this book), all stimulate the sense of speech for a child.

The Sense of Another's Thoughts

Children (and adults) have the ability to sense another's thoughts (believe it or not!). Thoughts create energy waves, either positive or negative, and they ripple into the environment. We have all walked into a room, and been hit with an uncomfortable feeling. We can sense when someone does not want to be at work, or at a social event, even though they are not saying so. Thoughts are living things, like speech, and therefore we need to keep our thoughts as positive, loving and non-judgmental as possible around babies and children – and everyone!

Once, in my playgroup, a little girl really drew my attention. On a number of occasions throughout the morning I thought, 'What a marvelous, beautiful child she is, so beautiful, free and unique.' At the end of the session, without warning, she leapt off her mother's lap and into my arms in a spontaneous loving embrace. Her mummy was amazed, explaining that the child was usually quiet and shy in nature, and she had never done anything like this before. I knew in my heart that she had 'heard' me. I now try and approach all children with this attitude of love for their uniqueness. Loving and non-judgmental thoughts are 'real'.

When there has been a battle of wills, harsh words or stressful parenting moments, be aware of the breath, and move on. Forgive and forget (simple but not always easy), try to create healthy family thought patterns again as soon as possible after the event.

The Sense of Another's 'I'

Babies and young children experience a strong sense of another person's warmth and integrity. They absorb another person's energy, as if it is their own. Some babies are very sensitive and only feel comfortable in their parents' sense of 'I' (in other words, their parent's arms). Try to be understanding; do not pressure unhappy babies to be passed around. Rather than having to kiss Aunty Betty, a young child can give a high five or a wave. Be the best person that you can be around children; they are absorbing everything about us. Integrity counts: children feel it.

Don't tell lies to children, for example, pretending there are no biscuits left in the tin when you do not want a child to have one. Children can sense the truth. White lies inadvertently teach children to tell white lies too. Be honest with children. (Father Christmas is real, the Spirit of Saint Nicholas!) If a child enquires about an adult conversation, simply state, 'This is adult talk, not for you to worry about.' Foster honesty, it creates family trust.

In *The Developing Child: The First Seven Years* (WECAN), Dr Helmut von Kugelman says:

The first law of childhood is that the small child's whole body is a sense organ, open to any and every impression. The child is extremely sensitive to the immediate surroundings. A smile, an expression of love, a tender word (unequal sources of warmth and strength), colors, shapes, arrangement of things, and positive thoughts of people in the surroundings – all shape and form the child as do nervousness, senseless acts and outbursts of temper...

He continues:

There are three different kinds of 'sustenance' that nourish children and become part of them: food, the air they breathe and the sense impressions from the world around them.

All the chapters of *Happy Child, Happy Home* that enhance communication, connection and creativity in family life also enhance children's twelve senses – and adults' senses too! Relax (remember thought patterns!): no one is perfect. These ideas create a growing consciousness, for next time, and next time, and next time. And so it goes.

Reflection

Watching TV sitting alone and still uses two senses.
What about the other ten?

How Does a House Become a Home?
The Seven Life Processes

The Twelve Senses help us to relate to the outside world. The Seven Processes of Life take place within the body. Rudolf Steiner described Seven Life Processes: breathing, warming, nourishing, secreting, maintaining, growing and generating. A home can be compared to a living entity. By understanding what makes a human body healthy, we can understand a healthy home. By being conscious of what the Seven Life Processes might mean in connection with our home and family, transformation occurs.

Breathing

Air is essential. Open windows and allow fresh air to circulate.

Breathing is a rhythmical activity, in and out breaths; let's match the breathing rhythm of our bodies in our homes. Too much activity, hurriedness and over-stimulation is like fast and rapid breathing, which is a sign of anxiety.

A house becomes a home by being together. A home requires time spent in it to relax, play and snuggle, to, in a word, connect. In Chapter One – Positive Family Rhythms, we cover the process of breathing well in our homes. The rhythmical 'breathing' sense of a day: greetings, meal times, rest times, soothing bedtimes.

Something to Try

Why wait to be stressed? Consciously breathe now!

Warming

Besides the physical ways of warming a home – the heating appliances – there may be atmospheric candles, open fires, salt lamps, hot-water bottles, the warm colours of rugs and sofas. Also, clothes, bedding and the texture and feel of toys give warmth.

Warmth equates to love and interest for each family member (and household pets). Genuine relationships are built on warmth – soul warmth. Warm-hearted people have a great effect on children. How do we feel when the warmth of the Sun comes out after rain? When we receive a cold shoulder or a friendly warm smile?

The process of breathing and warming interconnect. A slow, connecting rhythm (at certain times of the day) creates warmth in family life.

Nourishing

We are warm and rhythmically breathing; however, the body still requires nourishment. Choose foods for optimal vitamin and mineral intake. Prepare meals together; communicate around the family dinner table.

Nourishment also refers to the digestion process. Overstimulation (a hurried life) is very difficult for digestion, as are critical comments and unkind words. Nourish each other with kind words and warm deeds.

On subtle levels, beauty nourishes the home: seasonal table treasures, flowers, the songs and stories we create – all these nourish the heart and home.

Secreting

Sifting and sorting, retaining what is essential, while rejecting the inessential – this is secreting. So, here's to tidiness and cleanliness, less clutter and dust. I love a spring clean! Secreting is excreting what is useless: items and objects, yes, but also family habits and patterns. Secreting allows for transformation. Prioritise what is important in life and let go of habits and objects that do not serve the family's highest good. Observe the home, sense the process of secretion and allow for change.

Maintaining

Ongoing maintenance makes for a long-term healthy body and the same is true for the home environment. Be conscious of maintaining; write down the Seven Life Processes, and stick them on the fridge. Check in from time to time: any maintenance required? I don't mean just the general maintenance to your home, such as changing the washers on leaky taps. Perhaps look a bit deeper.

Growing

Let's celebrate as children become taller, measure them on a height chart. Record babies' milestones and celebrate children's birthdays (remember the birthday spiral and birthday table from Chapter Two). By maintaining the Seven Life Processes, growth occurs. Families who do things together, grow together! The collective positive memory bank expands, and the house grows into a home.

Generating

The final stage in the Seven Life Processes is generating (or maturing). In his lecture 'Working with the Life Processes' (available on www.johnallison.com.au), John Allison draws on his background in Steiner-Waldorf education when he tells us:

Generating results from the work that we do – a previously unimagined future blossoms into a new world of possibilities.

What we generate in our home and family life will have a positive effect on our children now, and for generations to come.

Reflection

Every home is different, both in its building materials (bricks, wood, mortar and such) and in family dynamics. All buildings and family set-ups can be nurtured by observing and working with the Seven Life Processes. Every house, unit, flat, tent, campervan or igloo can become a home.

A Word From a Dad – Michael

I once heard that a room with curved boards between the walls and the ceiling lowers our blood pressure by several points. Apparently it's more like a cave. Our environment can change our blood pressure.

Real Life Story
Louise – Touch Between Parent and Child

I was recently at a family wedding and at the reception I saw a mum giving her twenty-something son a shoulder massage. The picture was one of comfortable ease and natural connection. I could sense this massage had been done a thousand times while the son was growing up. The fact that her son was still comfortable with her touch (and in a public place!) was heartwarming. I felt a little envy!

Real Life Story
Michael – Secretion

Secretion is the 'process by which substances are produced and discharged from a cell, gland or organ for a function in the organism' (Oxford English Dictionary). In other words, we recognise what exists as valuable, but just don't want it here, thanks. The gall bladder produces bile and delivers it nicely into the gut and all is well, but if there is a blockage, the same substance and process becomes extremely painful! Ask anyone with gallstones. We need to move that blockage. Another analogy is putting vegetable peelings into the compost to make valuable material in the garden. The peelings need to be shifted from the kitchen to do any good and not to be in the way. Thich Nhut Hahn recommends we compost anger and fear: they are fine in themselves, just not here, thanks.

Checklist – Twelve Senses and Seven Life Processes

1. Find your child's 'soft spot' and give them the precious gift of touch.

2. When a baby or child cries, ask 'What is affecting their sense of life?'

3. Remember that movement is the key to a 'well-balanced' child.

4. Include the following balancing activities during childhood: rocking-chairs; riding on the knee and shoulders; playground rides, trikes and swings; balancing on walls; and the childhood games of skipping and hopscotch.

5. Look into children's eyes – a smiling face nurtures the senses of sight.

6. What's that smell? A cake? Remind children to smell the roses! Surround them with natural scents.

7. Stimulate children's taste buds with real foods (a healthy habit for life).

8. Keep children warm; their bodies are busy growing.

9. All sounds stimulate the nervous system; what daily sounds does your child hear? Is there too much noise?

10. Be aware of the quality of your speech around children. Sing songs and tell stories with them – they love your voice!

11. What are our thought patterns? Thoughts are like words – they can be felt by others.

12. Children sense a person's integrity. Being 'present' with your child is a present.

13. How does a house become a home? By balancing the breathing 'rhythm' of activity and rest, of being busy and being connected!

14. Warmth is a wonderful sensation, especially soul warmth.

15. What provides nourishment in your home?

16. Discover the joys of spring cleaning: secrete and transform!

17. Does your home require any maintenance to the Seven Life Processes?

18. Families who spend time together grow together.

19. Generate a positive environment at home.

Chapter Nine
Creative Discipline

Children are educated by what the grown-up is and not by his talk.

CARL JUNG

Laying the Foundation for a Happy and Settled Child

When I offer my Conscious Parenting classes, more parents enrol for 'Creative Discipline' than for any other topic. However, it is by attending to the other aspects of family life – including positive rhythms, healthy eating, and creative play – that we minimise the issues and problems that require Creative Discipline.

Let's take rhythm: if children don't get enough sleep – time to relax, rest, play at home, time for cuddles, softness and love – they become tired, grumpy, overly sensitive and clingy. They cry easily.

Is food contributing to energy highs and lows and erratic, excitable behaviour? Additives – colours, flavours, flavour enhancers and preservatives – are linked to hyperactivity in children. You can find more information on Sue Dengate's website (www.fedup.com.au).

When children are playing, are they getting overstimulated by noise and action toys? Do they get more active and 'high'? If they are sitting in front of hours of superhero images and television, do they then fly around the room and get easily bored, lacking the imaginative skills for prolonged and creative play?

Is there an enriching imaginative play corner in the heart of your home, and similar spaces in the garden? These have a profound effect on a child's mood. Can young children join in with all the household chores: chopping, cooking, washing, and shopping? Little hands love to be included, interacting with parents, and it keeps them out of mischief!

Laying the foundation for a calm and happy child

If you are attending to all these aspects of family life, there will of course still be times when children display inappropriate behaviour, and that is when you will need Creative Discipline techniques. I have ten techniques to suggest and explain. These are resources you can choose to use when need arises.

The 'Least Restrictive First' System

I started my teaching career working with special needs students and specialised in teaching children with autism and Asperger's Syndrome. These experiences taught me about children's behaviours (and autistic children can really throw tantrums!). The school I was lucky enough to teach in had a wonderful behavioural system called 'Least Restrictive First'. There were a number of different interventions we could make with children who were behaving in a difficult manner. The 'Least Restrictive First' system encouraged us to start with the gentlest of these interventions and only use our more stringent methods if the gentler ones had failed to change behaviour. Over the past twenty years while I have been teaching in primary, special needs and Rudolf Steiner settings and leading Waldorf playgroups, I have had, and still have, ample opportunities to practise the positive techniques from this discipline system on lovely children. Plus I have two of my own, now twelve and fourteen years of age. I have adapted and developed, the 'Least Restrictive First' method and call my set of ten techniques 'Creative Discipline'.

The 'Least Restrictive First' method was part of the curriculum to develop appropriate behaviours. New behaviours had to be actively taught and encouraged. This is also the case with toddlers. Can you guess the root word of 'discipline'? It stems from 'disciple' and means simply 'to teach'.

What is Creative Discipline?

Creative Discipline is a bag of useful tools for teaching children appropriate behaviours, and for transforming challenges in a positive manner. An appropriate behaviour is achieved or an undesired behaviour is stopped. How we find our way there is a matter of creative choice.

There are many possible approaches when it comes to discipline; I am choosing one that empowers both parent and child, is fun, understanding, centred and loving – well most of the time anyway!

I explain ten techniques for Creative Discipline below.

1. Ask The Question 'Why?'

What is happening for the child? When young children display inappropriate behaviours, the first response – rather than pointing a finger – can be to ponder the question 'Why?' Ask yourself, not your children. Behaviours are a means of communicating. Are the children tired or hungry? Is your child's body asking to move out of the car seat or pushchair? Do the children need a slower pace, perhaps, and special time with a parent? (In Chapter One I mentioned Steve Biddulph's claim that '75 per cent of discipline problems are caused from the hurry that parents are in.')

When pondering the question 'Why?' the child's age plays a large factor: just what are realistic expectations? What do we need to teach? Children require patience and repetition to master new social skills. Take the time to watch and listen to them. Are children in fact being creative and inquisitive? Their loudness or messiness may be annoying, but perhaps it is not purposely disruptive?

If behaviours repeat, keep a diary to note down challenging moments, and aim to answer the question 'Why?' What are the triggers? Aim to see disruptive behaviour as fascinating, and to remain calm. Stand in your children's shoes, see and feel how their world is for them.

The Mud Pot Story

There was once a young boy playing and exploring in his garden. He began to play with some mud near his sandpit. It worked so well with water, he made a ball and put his thumb in, and before his eyes it became a beautiful pot. In the kitchen, Mum was cleaning the floor. The boy was so excited that he had to show the person he loved the most his new treasure.

He went skipping through the open kitchen door, 'Mum!' he shouted running up to her. His shoes were still on and a trail of mud followed him. His mother did not see the pot in his outstretched hands or his smiling face, only the footprints on her clean kitchen floor. She screamed, which stopped the boy in his tracks, his pulse beginning to race. 'Get out, look at all the mud you have brought in!'

The boy turned away in shame, and went outside alone. His mother never did see the pot. Biting back tears, the boy squashed it and put it back in the mud pile where it came from. Confused about being happy one moment and so ashamed the next, he never made a pot to show his mother again.

How different would it be if his mother had asked what he wanted, and replied, 'A lovely pot, let's put it on the window sill outside, and then clean up these footprints together. Look at your giant muddy feet!'

How often do we blame, confuse and shame our children, not understanding the real message of their behaviour? I put my hand up high here; I have misunderstood my children's creative actions and felt angry. I have witnessed their faces fall from cheerful to sudden confusion. Try asking 'Why?' to see what a child's behaviour is really indicating. Is the child really meaning to cause trouble? Maybe they are expressing a need to lead a less hurried life, or showing you a special pot?

After asking 'Why?' the ideal next step when dealing with inappropriate behaviour is *redirection*.

2. Redirection: the Best Way

There are ten Creative Discipline techniques. Of them all, redirection is my most commonly used tool. There are three different ways to redirect a child's behavior: to action, to a new situation, to teach.

Redirect the Action

Identify the action a child is displaying and redirect it into a safe and positive play experience.

Scenario: a five-year-old is running inside at a social gathering.

Redirect the action of running: 'Can you run to that tree and back three times in the garden? I will watch from the window. Outside is a great place to run.'

Scenario: an eighteen-month-old is banging on the window with a hard object. (It makes a lovely sound!)

Redirect the action of banging: 'We bang on a drum, let's tap a wooden spoon on a saucepan. This is how we tap, well done, not on the window.'

Scenario: a two-year-old is throwing wooden blocks inside; they do look great flying through the air!

Redirect the action of throwing: place a basket nearby and hand your child a felt ball: 'We throw balls. Throw the ball into the basket, goal! Balls are for throwing, not blocks or toys; well done!'

Scenario: climbing indoors.

Redirect the action of climbing: you've guessed it, suggest climbing on the play equipment in the garden or park, or heading outside for some balancing fun.

Isolate the action, then show where that action can take place.

Redirect to a New Situation

When trying moments occur, a change of scene or activity can quickly change a child's mood and behaviour. Children tend to live in the moment, so redirecting to a new situation can sometimes enable them to leave difficulties behind completely.

Scenario: a three-year-old is tired but does not want to rest.

Redirect to a new resting scene or activity: throw a big bed sheet over the kitchen table to make a cosy den (include cushions and books). Or, start reading a story to big teddy on your bed; your child will soon follow.

Scenario: while on a play date, children are arguing over a toy.

Redirect to a new activity or play space: 'Who would like to come and help make popcorn for morning tea? Let's watch it pop?' Or 'Let's go into the garden and play in the sandpit.'

Scenario: children are upset about leaving a venue.

Redirect with a little tale or some pretend play: 'Look at that bird in the tree; it sounds like it's calling your names! Listen, Roger, Roger, Emma, Emma!'

Redirect to Teach

Parents can fall into the trap of reacting to undesirable behaviours by saying – often in a raised voice – 'Don't do...' or 'No...' or 'Stop it!' With this type of negative instruction, the child hears what not to do, but there is no guidance to teach the appropriate way of behaving (now and for the future). Each time a child displays an unwanted behaviour, an opportunity arises to teach the child how to live in the world. We learn not by getting it right, but by making mistakes.

The most commonly used phrasing at times of inappropriate behaviour is the negative: 'Do not hit!', 'Stop running!' But the child still hears the words 'running' and 'hit'! Instead, emphasise the positive instruction and the verb that describes the desired behaviour: 'Use clever hands!', 'Walking inside! (Running is for outside.)' We need to state what we expect children to do. This correct behaviour can then be practised together.

Scenario: a child is pulling a cat's tail.

Redirect to teach care of a cat: 'We stroke a pussy cat like this.' (Demonstrate.) 'He loves to be treated kindly and softly. Great, you are doing such a good job, being gentle. He loves that!'

Scenario: a young child hits a playmate to get a toy.

Redirect to teach solutions: say 'Hands down' in a calm assertive manner. Tell the child to use words to get a turn. Find a similar toy to play with. Let the child help you find a timer to play a turn-taking game. 'When the bell rings it's mine!' Model an apology and demonstrate 'gentleness' with friends. Empower children to say 'Stop! I don't like it' when they are hurt.

A Suggestion

Before your children have a play date at home, go through their toys and allow them to put their special things away in a cupboard. Only leave out the toys they are happy to share. This solves a lot of play date issues.

If arguing begins, ask your child, 'Is this a special toy and shall we put it up high?' Explain simply to the friend, 'Do you have special toys? What are they?' 'This is a special toy too; let's find something else to play with.'

If play dates at home become overly argumentative (if there are meltdowns), plan to meet up with friends in a neutral play location, such as the local park. For two-to-five-year-olds this can be much easier (a happy change of environment).

Explain gentleness throughout the week with toys, and chat about what makes a good friend, introducing words for simple emotions: 'Sam does not like to be hit, it makes him sad.' Talk about how clever hands are: look at the four fingers and thumb. Have the children help you think of all the things 'clever' hands can do. Reiterate: 'Clever hands don't hit; remember to use your words.' Tell a story about a dog who cleverly learnt to use her bark, not her teeth!

Each time children display a challenging behaviour there is an opportunity to teach them. This kind of intervention is subtle, but powerful. Children (even teenagers!) are more open to guidance when they are redirected to positive behaviours. They learn what to do next time. This is teaching life skills!

3. Change the Environment

As well as redirecting children who are behaving inappropriately, we have the tool of changing the environment.

Scenario: a child doesn't want to get in the car.

Change the environment in the car: hang a mobile and buy some special car pockets for favourite toys and new special books that are just for car journeys.

Scenario: it's raining on a playgroup day so the children can't play outside after morning tea as they're used to.

Change the environment inside: give the room a new and special 'rainy day' feel. We move the sofas to face each other and throw a bedspread over them; the children climb in, and a parent reads to them. This keeps the session running smoothly.

Tip

Other solutions to car resistance include:

* Have a special tub of healthy treats to offer on car journeys.
* Encourage the child to look after teddy or dolly in the car.
* Play simple car games: sing a song, tell a story, or spot cars of particular colours out of the window.
* Listen for the seat belt to say 'Click!'
* Keep a bubble-pot and wand in the glove compartment. Blow and catch a few bubbles before starting the engine.

Remember also to ask 'Why?' and to assess how much time you are spending in the car. Are you attempting too many outings? Plan at least one or two home days a week.

Scenario: A child is afraid at night.

Change the environment of the bedroom: de-clutter and eliminate big dark shapes (the toy dog on the chair looks different in the dark). Leave a comforting night light on, and cocoon the bed with a silk hanging.

Keep a diary of difficult times and then brainstorm how to creatively change the environment to transform behaviours.

4. Say 'No!' in a Different Way

Children are natural explorers; they are new to the world and want to experience things – not necessarily things that are healthy for them or convenient for us. Parents usually say 'no' because they are hurried or the child's request is not safe or is not the best option at the time. It is possible, however, for parents to say 'no' by deferring gratification, offering an alternative choice, or redirecting to a new situation rather than simply saying 'no' and leaving the child feeling thwarted. These techniques are powerful tools for Creative Discipline.

If you say 'No' directly to young children, they find it difficult to process; their impulse has been denied. A reaction occurs, sometimes a tantrum. Techniques of delayed gratification, offering alternatives or redirecting their focus, can help avoid such reactions while still holding firm boundaries.

I find this is my most misunderstood Creative Discipline suggestion. By changing the word 'no', I definitely do not mean that you are, or should be, saying 'yes!' We must hold clear boundaries around suitable social behaviours, and around lifestyle choices like what to eat and how much TV to watch. (My children have had plenty of boundaries for these!)

I am not suggesting we never use the word 'no', but if we save it for critical situations, such as safety hazards, rather than using it repeatedly when children are exploring or are full of requests, then it will hold more power.

Here are some creative answers to common scenarios:

Child at breakfast time: 'Can I have a biscuit?'

Defer gratification: 'Yes darling – you can have a biscuit after breakfast for morning tea. Let's put it here on a special plate so that we remember, and get teddy to watch over it!' A toy watching over something is always fun!

Child asks for attention while you are busy: 'I want you to read me a story.'

Redirect by involving the child with the activity at hand, then spend time with them. 'Help me with the washing up, and then we will look at the book together.'

Child wants to stop and look at everything on a walk past the shops when you are in a hurry for an appointment.

Redirect the child by racing or moving like cheetahs. 'We can look in there another day; let's race now to the lights: ready steady go, let's run!'

Child in a shopping centre toyshop: 'I want a new Lego set and a torch I have seen!'

'What a great idea, let's put them on your Christmas list, let me write it down now.' Carry a pen and pad for this; make a fuss of taking a note. Children are very likely to have forgotten by Christmas time, or have asked for another five things!

Child: 'I want to watch TV'.

Offer alternatives: 'Your beautiful brain wants to move and play, let's set up a play shop.' Or 'Come and help me cook.' (Remember the play chart or photo book in Chapter Seven.)

Tantrums may still occur, but, with these Creative Discipline tools, they are far less frequent and severe. Move on quietly with the child, ignore the tantrum, and redirect. We can give our children solid boundaries and guide their lives without constant battles of wills.

By changing the word 'no' we actively teach children how to make future requests (when it's acceptable to eat a biscuit, what kind of ice lollies are allowed). This is a useful tool for life. As children grow older, 'no' can be used more often, with an explanation now they can understand. Note that older children will model these redirection techniques back to you, so that when you ask, 'Would you vacuum please,' you may hear, 'Yes, after I have...'

Something to Try

For a day, avoid the word 'no', and see what happens...

Parents tend to say 'no' because they have no time, or because the activity or food request is not aligned to their principles. Instead of saying 'no', tell your child when their request can be fulfilled, or suggest an alternative food or activity. This allows the child to be heard, and also teaches better choices for the future.

5. Games and Giggles

Playing little games can be a magic wand for achieving tasks with young children. It's a Creative Discipline technique that leads you directly to happiness and connection while getting things done.

For children who refuse to put on their socks, try saying: 'I am Sandy Sock and I love to eat toes! I eat them all the way up – look at that – all the way up to the ankle!' Or, for example, with pyjamas say, 'Can you put your pyjamas on by the time I make a cup of tea? Race you, ready steady go!' It's preferable that young children race a parent, but not each other. With sibling rivalry and only one winner, a meltdown may occur!

To feel relaxed in stressful moments, try a tickle from time to time. Most children cannot resist having a giggle. So when children stamp their feet and say 'no', say: 'I am going to tickle you!' Lightheartedness can be a very successful tool.

When you need to hurry, try 'Beat the Timer': 'Can you be dressed before the timer rings? Bet you can't!' Or fly like space rockets, not like slow pedal bikes.

When the cold weather arrives, so does the autumn gnome! When no one is looking, he takes all the t-shirts and shorts away. What is not in the clothes drawers cannot be asked for!

Remember 'Teethy Tales' from Chapter One? If hair brushing is becoming a strain, tell stories of what the hairs will do today.

Stories are a fun way to transform behaviours. If a child is pushing other children, tell a story about Rosie dog, who pushes his doggy friend Rufus away from the food bowl. Explain how sad Rufus feels. Include a solution in the story: Farmer Joe uses the oven timer to help them take turns at the food bowl. Everybody wins!

Don't worry about continuously thinking up new games. Children like the same game for seven years!

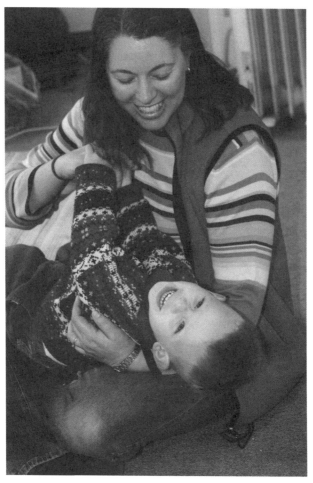

Change a mood – tickle!

Real Life Story

Veronica – Games for Troublesome Tasks,
Play for Times of Waiting

I'm blown away by the success of your getting-dressed strategies. I pretended the clothes were talking to my two-and-a-half-year-old daughter using lots of different voices. She loved it, and sat quietly on my lap while we played the talking clothes game. Wow! That beats the loggerhead stand-offs we've had the past months.

Then my daughter and four-year-old son had a ball playing restaurants. They co-operated beautifully on that while I had to do jobs quickly about the house and get ready for an outing.

6. The Power of Praise

Children do not require constant praising; it can lead to increased anxiety and to the need for adult approval, 'Am I doing the right thing now?' But praise can be a useful tool for transforming challenging behaviours. Isolate one or two positive behaviours that you would like to see again. Every time you see these behaviours, offer praise. Reinforce again at bedtime when you are having a cuddle: 'I was really pleased with the way you used your words and not your hands at playgroup today!'

I use the power of praise in my classroom. If the class is beginning to get disruptive I highlight one child sitting still and paying attention, and I praise them verbally in front of the class. This has a knock-on effect on behaviour, so I praise another child and then another, and soon everyone is looking and listening.

At times of challenging behaviour, redirect to the appropriate behaviour and then praise. You are likely to see the desired behaviour again.

Remember to praise the behaviour, rather than the child: 'great sharing' rather than 'good girl'.

In addition, label the unacceptable behavior and not the child: 'hitting hurts' or 'hitting is not acceptable', rather than 'naughty girl'.

'I love you' and 'beautiful boy' and 'my darling girl' are not praise but terms of endearment, and cannot be said enough.

Something to Think About

At teacher training college I was taught a theory of labels that suggests if we assign a child a particular label in their family or the classroom or in their community, this will have a powerful effect on their sense of identity. If you call a child a troublemaker, he or she is likely to become one. But this power of labels can function in positive as well as negative ways, so it can be a creative tool for giving a child a strong sense of positive qualities to aspire to and, through this, changing their behaviour.

7. Giving Children a Positive Role

Children love to be given specific roles, and to be acknowledged as useful. Fiery children particularly require tasks and challenges. Are there items they can carry, things they can look after or a job they can help with?

A kindergarten assistant shared her observations with me, which demonstrated how transformative it can be to offer a specific role to a child when he or she is doing things with adults:

I was in a hardware shop at the weekend. In one aisle there were two boys of similar ages with their dads. Both were out shopping, but one boy was miserable and the other was happy. The difference was that the happy boy was included. The outing had been made special by involving him as much as possible. He was pushing a little barrow, chatting to his dad and following directions to find items. He was his dad's helper. The miserable boy was tagging along behind while his dad growled, 'Hurry up!'

A Suggestion

Give strong-willed children tasks (little leadership roles). 'Can you get the mail in your special postbag?' 'Help me chop the fruit for our plate.' Use and extend their 'will' to be helpful, strong, and useful – to achieve tasks. Involve them.

---

8. Parents as Role models

Parents' mode of discipline is itself a model for how we want children to behave when stressed or when dealing with conflict. The way you behave, especially at difficult moments, is a resource children can draw on when they face difficulties. Your actions and mode of being are more powerful than any words of advice. It is paradoxical to see a parent shout, 'No shouting!' or to hit a child as a response to the child's rough behaviour. Children made to sit isolated from others can put up a protective wall. If shut in a closed room, their screams can, at times, be primal and unnerving.

Rather than resorting to isolating or shouting at children, try to talk reasonably, teach positively, and lovingly guide. It is difficult to stay calm always and still be assertive (I know) but if you can, then by assimilation these habits become life communication skills for children too. It is a wonderful experience, after years of role-modelling, to see children treat each other with respect and hear our positive manner reflected by them. Children brought up with Creative Discipline techniques know how to communicate well and care for others throughout their lives. This is powerful knowledge.

9. Clever Choices

A choice between two selected items can help a child comply with a task. Choosing allows children their own feeling of power, but the two options are controlled by the parents. This is a very helpful tool when getting dressed and at snack time!

Scenario: a child is asking for an inappropriate snack item while shopping.
    Offer a different choice between two healthy snack items: 'You can have grapes or a fruity stick.' If the child still asks for the first unhealthy snack, repeat the choice of two. Then limit the choice, 'Grapes or nothing at all, your choice!'

Scenario: a child does not want to put on a dressing gown in wintertime.
    Offer a choice of the dressing gown or a jumper (or even a dress-up option: cape, cloak, poncho, armour).

Clever choices can be part of how we phrase quiet removal. If sharing is difficult and if redirection to another toy or situation isn't working, then quiet removal can be put to the child in a way that makes it clear that the outcome of this situation is their choice, but the inappropriate behaviour is not acceptable: 'Take turns with the toy or put it up high? Your choice.'

10. Quiet Removal

The most restrictive intervention when I was working with autistic children was 'time out'; this was used as a last resort. The last technique of Creative Discipline is quiet removal, which is not the same as time out, but has the similarity that we only use it after the other Creative Discipline techniques have been tried and a challenging behaviour still requires modifying.

When, after redirecting, changing the environment or playing a game, a young child is still displaying inappropriate behaviour, state the positive way to behave and allow for one last chance. If the child's behaviour is still unacceptable, then quietly remove her or him or the fought-over toy from the situation. 'You need to stay with me until I know John is safe. No hitting; everyone needs to feel safe.' This is quiet removal: quietly taking the toy or child away from the situation, while stating the positive way to behave.

It is at these times that tested parents and carers may overreact. Try to remember that quiet removal is a useful tool.

Together with quiet removal (with children who are verbal and able to understand), I use 'thinking time' to make amends, if the child needs to calm down. During the 'thinking time', the child stays near me – he or she is not sent to a corner or their room – but is away from others and their play activity. This is not a quick sorry through gritted teeth, but thinking of a way to make the hurt child happy again. If the child is unable to do this, we can step in and model a caring idea. This creates a clean sheet, before the next issue arises!

The purposes of quiet removal are: to remove the child if he or she is unsafe to others, to settle his or her emotions, to allow him or her to become more reflective about positive behaviours, and finally to reintroduce him or her into the group.

From four years of age on, when there has been conflict and a child is upset, I guide by bringing the two children involved together. I ask the hurt child to say to the other child 'I did not like it when you took my toy. It made me feel sad.' The other child usually tells their side of the story. (There *are* often two sides!) The children can, when assisted by our guidance, say sorry, make amends and find a solution.

Creative Discipline in Practice: Answering Two Common Questions from Parents

1. How can I help my child to listen and follow through on a request?

Once babies become toddlers they start to refer to themselves as 'I'. They will shift to saying 'I want a drink', rather than 'Johnny wants a drink'. This signals the dawning of consciousness in the child that she or he is a separate person: I am myself and may not agree with the choices made for me. This is the child's sense of self and will developing. Let's celebrate – this is not the 'terrible twos', but the 'terrific twos'!

Understand that the mode of refusal – 'no!' – can be an age and stage. I remember a funny cartoon of a two-year-old child being asked 'What's your name?' The reply was 'no!' It doesn't matter what the question is, the answer will be 'no!' for a toddler (and for a teenager!). This is an important stage. It helps children set boundaries for themselves.

For young children, perhaps keep a diary and note the times of day when a defiant 'no!' is voiced, as there may be a pattern. Create positive family rhythms to make the daily tasks of meal times, rest times and bed times full of connection and fun. Check how much control you are asking for. (Honestly, are you being an army sergeant?) Don't sweat the small stuff.

What can you do when 'no!' is in the air? Try these steps:

* Approach the child.
* Touch to gain her or his attention.
* Use the key word: 'Listen...'
* Give a short explanation of what needs to be done and why.
* Repeat your request calmly three times if necessary. 'Stop, listen...'
* Make sure your body language is saying 'I am not going away!'

> *Reflection*
>
> Invest in family connection. Connection between parents and children creates greater power to transform behaviours.

Sometimes meet children halfway. This allows for a cooperative win–win situation. 'Ok, I will put on one shoe and you can do the other.' 'I will pick up the toy cars and you can pick up the Lego.' Young children are looking for opportunities to do things for themselves.

Praise when the job is done: 'Great listening – high five!' Reinforce the key word 'Listen!' Praise again later in the day and share the good news with loved ones. 'Sally is a great listener; she helped to tidy her toys straightaway today.'

Is an activity finishing soon? Give ample time for children to adjust. 'Five minutes and we will pack away.' 'Two minutes and we finish playing to go to Kindergarten.' 'One minute, one more thing to play with.' This helps with transition times (leaving a play date, park or home play). Children live in the moment and find it hard to pack away when a game is gripping. Leaving a note on the toy can help: 'Jenny will be back after playgroup, no one touch!'

Count down in a firm voice: 'Three, two and one!' I use this in classrooms. When leaving a park or playground, make the motion of moving on as if the child is following, while keeping a safe eye on your child.

Remember clever choices between two options you have selected can help during defiant moments. 'The jumper or your coat, your choice to be warm?' If you still get a refusal, limit the choice, 'Your jumper or stay inside?' When an activity is not safe for your child or others, teach the safe way to behave. If you are ignored, again, offer a choice of two options. 'Play safely or we leave, what do you want to do?' Follow through in a calm, assertive manner.

Try empathising: 'I know you love to play diggers. I too find interesting things wonderful and hard to leave. You can play again before tea.' Explain what is coming up next and also when play can happen again.

You can also try using the child's empathy for your own situation. 'Help me out, I'd like to be on time for the doctor, or the doctor will be cross!' (said in funny voice).

Humour can alleviate children's moods and ours! Stamp your foot and say: 'Whatever you do, do NOT put your coat on, do not!' Your child will be surprised if you say the opposite of what you have been asking for. Keep it light, when hearing 'no'. Maybe tickle and chase until the job is done!

Tell stories about helping and not helping: 'The Little Red Hen' is a great one. None of Little Red Hen's farm animal companions will help with collecting or grinding the wheat or baking the cake, but they all want to eat the cake, to which the hen replies, 'No, not a crumb! You did not help when asked to collect the wheat, grind the wheat or bake the cake, so you shall not eat the cake!'

Explain the natural consequences of not listening and listening. 'If we don't leave now, we won't have time to...' 'Toys left on the floor can be stepped on and often break.' Talk about simple emotions that will be the consequences of particular actions: 'Emily (the kinder teacher) will be happy when everyone arrives on time. She can start the day with everyone together. Let's see her smile!'

Have reasonable expectations – try to only insist upon a few things a day (being on time for playgroup, nursery or school; packing away toys). Follow the tips above and stay calm: a quiet and assertive voice is more powerful than shouting, bribing or pleading. Threats and bribes require increased management. The children build resistance, as well as inner resentment, and empty threats lead to poor listening skills.

It is important to develop listening skills and responsiveness in our children. It requires patient, firm and loving teaching, and it will benefit our children's overall development, and our sanity!

Something to Try

Contemplate an adult who you particularly admired and liked growing up – a teacher, aunt or parent. What qualities did they display around children?

2. My two children always argue over toys – What can I do?

Squabbles are part and parcel of any sibling relationship. Conflict is inevitable, and is not a bad thing when we understand it as an opportunity for learning a new skill. Here are some practical tips for when those little voices shout, 'Mine, I had it first!' Most of these will work for play date squabbles as well as sibling squabbles.

If it's needed, allow older children special time away from a young toddler. Block off an area where they can play with their toys without disturbance. If children get upset with a toddler who is interfering with their play, ask, 'Do you want special time away by yourselves to play uninterrupted?' Allow older siblings to have their smaller toys on a high shelf that only they can access. When tensions are flying, suggest that older children relax with 'special time'.

If a toy is really special, for example a toy cash register, and is becoming a battleground for turns, buy another one (try a secondhand shop). One for each child means far fewer headaches!

Set up scenes that encourage social play together between siblings: farm yards, car mats, a shop, a home corner. Think of scenes from the real world. This will encourage play that develops social, communication and problem-solving skills.

Sharing is not a natural tendency for two and three year olds. Attachments to personal toys can be very strong; I liken their feelings to those of an adult getting a new car and a friend grabs the keys to go for a drive!

Show children ways of resolving conflict, such as finding a similar toy, or using a timer to help with turn-taking. If you are showing turn-taking, the child who had the toy first goes first. Or if prior possession is unclear, a game of 'Which hand holds the object behind my back?' or 'Pick the longest stick!' or tossing a coin is a fun way to decide who goes first.

If these strategies don't work, ask the child who owns the toy, 'Are you going to take turns or will I put this one up high as a special toy?' If the toy is not owned by any one child, simply state to both, 'Take turns or I will put the toy up high.' (This is quiet removal.)

Model how to ask for a turn: 'Please may I have a turn' Encourage children to share. Praise when you see this behaviour. With younger children, practise 'sharing' with teddy: 'Teddy's turn, your turn, Teddy's turn, your turn!'

If turn taking is difficult on a certain day, redirect to a more neutral activity (make a den under the table with a big cloth, or play outside).

Tell a (made-up) story at bedtime of how an animal learnt to share.

After being shown by an adult, over time older children learn to instigate a solution for themselves. When squabbles arise, the adult can say 'Work it out together, think of a way that makes you both happy.' It's lovely to see them come up with an idea.

Tip

When my twelve-year-old daughter's voice changes and stress is in the air, I remind her to breathe.

'I am breathing!' she says.

'Breathe deeply!' I reply, while modelling a deep breath. This calms me down too! It works to settle us, and gives us both practice in a stress-reduction technique.

Perfect Parent, Perfect Child – No such thing!

Remember that no child or parent is perfect, and neither should we be, as it is our mistakes that help us to learn and grow. As for the child, what a difficult thing it would be to live up to parent perfection!

Parenting can be like a dance: two steps forward and one step back. Be conscious of how things worked out during and after each incident with your child, how your heart really feels in each moment. Understand where you could have parented more positively to change inappropriate behaviours. Remember the ten Creative Discipline tools, and make plans to try a different response tomorrow...

Understanding a child's temperament is a very useful accompaniment to Creative Discipline, on to Chapter Ten...

A Word from a Dad – Michael

Thinking about discipline: don't use a mallet to brush off a fly.

A Word from Seven-year-old Jayson

When I was little I liked to be a forklift at tidy-up time. Mummy pressed a button to turn me on. It made packing away exciting. Daddy swirled me round as a helicopter for bedtime; I looked forward to that game each night.

Real Life Story
Joseph – The Magic Claw

My 'magic claw' has helped with my children's defiance over many years. If my children say 'no' when it is time for bed or to another request, the magic claw comes out to play! The claw is essentially my hand, arm and fingers outstretched ready to poke, tickle and coerce children on their way. I am smiling while I do this, it's a game – so giggles and shrieks occur. The magic claw tickles, with an edge of danger. It works every time!

Real Life Story

Ryan and Jacqui – Mouths are for Eating, Kissing, Blowing Bubbles

While our eighteen-month-old boy has a gorgeous, fun-loving temperament seventy per cent of the time, his ever-increasing tantrums and biting were of great concern to us.

After attending Lou's Creative Discipline workshop, we started implementing her ideas as soon as we arrived home. We saw positive results in his behaviour almost immediately. Through recognising and making the necessary changes to *our* behaviour and actions, most tantrum-provoking episodes have been removed from our days. And in the event we start heading down that path, we now possess the skills to quickly steer things in another direction. PHEW! We've seen great progress.

We reinforce that mouths are for eating, kissing, blowing bubbles and talking – not biting.

We now enjoy more laughter-filled, quality playtime together, and still tend to life's other responsibilities. I feel like we're not only bringing the balance back, but also helping our son create a strong, healthy foundation for the rest of his life. And I feel happier within myself while getting to be a positive role model!

Checklist – Creative Discipline

1. Revise the earlier chapters in this book. Positive rhythms, healthy, additive-free food and imaginative play all positively affect the behaviour of children.

2. What does *discipline* mean? To teach!

3. Ask the question 'Why?' It's wonderful to discover the root cause of a behaviour.

4. Redirect the action: where does it belong – outside?

5. Redirect to change a child's mood.

6. State the positive action when you ask your child to change behaviour, rather than talking about the negative action.

7. Challenging issue? Can you change the environment around the child to help?

8. Transform the word 'no' when responding to a child's request and still hold the boundaries.

9. Games and giggles work – try a game rather than a growl.

10. Offer clever choices between two options. The child feels empowered while the parents are still determining the overall direction.

11. What is our behaviour modelling for children?

12. The technique of quiet removal is best left until last, after other Creative Discipline tools have been tried.

13. Keep a diary of challenging moments and write down ideas.

14. Visit me on www.skiptomylouparenting.com for further Creative Discipline tips and to find my earlier book, *Turning Tears into Laughter: Creative Discipline for the Toddler and Preschool Years*.

Chapter Ten
The Four Temperaments

All the world's a stage,
And all the men and women merely players,
They have their exits and their entrances,
And one man in his time plays many parts,
His act being seven ages.

WILLIAM SHAKESPEARE, *AS YOU LIKE IT*

Know the Child, See the Child, Hear the Child

The concept of temperaments is over 2000 years old, dating back to ancient Greek times. The Greeks compared four main character types with the elements earth, air, fire and water. This knowledge of temperaments was used in ancient medicine.

Rudolf Steiner uses the Four Temperaments to understand the human being and stages of life, and to assist teachers in educating different children. The Four Temperaments are: sanguine, choleric, melancholic and phlegmatic, and I discuss them in detail in this chapter. Steiner's insights are invaluable for helping parents to understand their children.

Family Dynamics

Although siblings share the same parents, heritage and upbringing, they can be very different in temperament. Similarly, a quietly spoken, sensitive parent may have a willful, loud and boisterous child. And a fun-loving, outgoing parent may have a shy and anxious child.

Know the child, see the child, hear the child

The lesson for all of us is to learn to love and truly accept our children's temperaments in a non-judgmental manner. This in turn allows our children to develop and become the best people they can be. One temperament is not better or worse than another. All temperaments have both positive and negative traits. The negative traits are not to be suppressed but supported, to bring about a balance of the whole developing child. This fosters living in the world in a harmonious way.

In *Understanding Your Temperament* (Sophia Books), Dr Gilbert Childs states:

...no one should on any account attempt to change the
temperament your child already possesses. If you do
try you will only succeed in confusing and bewildering
the child. Their temperament is built into their very
constitution, and any attempt to change it would be equal
to resorting to plastic surgery...

At What Age Can We See Children's Temperaments?

Until the age of seven, children are still working with hereditary
patterns and past influences. With the change of teeth, children
begin to develop their own sense of 'I', their own sense of Self or
character. At fourteen, their own separate Self can be seen clearly.
When we witness their Self in their twenties, we see the influence
of family to a lesser and lesser extent.

We may see glimpses of a child's temperament when younger
than seven (especially if it is different to the stages of life).
However, it is not until the change of teeth that it becomes
more apparent, and then again at fourteen, and by 21 it is clearly
shining.

Please do not put people and children in temperament boxes;
this chapter is a loose guide. Also, refrain from mentioning
children's perceived temperaments in their presence. Once a
child hears the name of a temperament and it is reinforced as
their own, they may become it. It is important for children to
express their temperament and grow through it. A spiritual aim is
to balance all four temperaments in our character.

Temperament Types

We have four temperaments within us, but one plays out
dominantly. A secondary one will also be prominent, with the
other two playing a much more minor role. Our temperament
determines our basic character: how we approach the world, how
we relate to others and ourselves, and how we act in different
situations.

A poem found in an old German convent sheds light on the Four Temperament types. It is a story of a stone on the path:

Lightly he springs o'er the stone,
The sanguine one;
Quick and with grace,
If he trips, he cares not,
With a laugh he continues his race.

Grimly the choleric kicks at the stone,
Hurling it out of his way.
As he exults in his strength
See his eyes flash fire.

Now the phlegmatic appears
And pensively slows down his step.
'If this stone will not move from the path
I must go round and all will be well.'

Silently stands by the stone,
Brooding, the melancholy one,
Grumbling and plunged in despair
At his eternally lasting doom.

Sanguine

Sanguines are the extroverts. Their attention focuses in the outer world and social situations. They are constantly aware of what's going on around them (looking for the new and interesting). Think of a sanguine type as the wind, blowing here and there, ever changing! The sanguine temperament's colour is yellow and its element is air. The body type is slim with a heart shaped or oval face. They have a lightness of step. While this type is re-energised through being with people, they may also find they need grounding while in social situations and afterwards. Being 'scattered' is a great descriptive term for the sanguine state and for their tendency in social groups.

Sanguines are good-natured, with many friends. (Life and soul of the party!) They are optimistic and flexible, sensitive and kind, wishing others well. They rarely hold a grudge for long, but if they lose respect for someone it is never forgotten. This is not a bad thing – for a socially-open person this provides their intuitive boundary.

They are great conversationalists and storytellers.

On the flip side, sanguines tend to be impressionable (including being prone to hearsay and gossip), imitative (they take in and copy attributes around them), excitable and unreliable. They don't easily retain information, having short powers of concentration but bucket-loads of intuition and imagination. Experience is their best teacher, and this temperament will gain wisdom with age. (Sanguines will make the best grandparents!) They love change, so find it difficult to stick to a task – close enough is near enough with chores!

Sanguine Children – Butterfly Children

Do you have a butterfly type? These children often flit from one activity to the next with their feet hardly touching the ground.

The butterfly type lives in the moment in their magical world, so give them the freedom of time. Don't get upset if, when on the way to their shoes, they find other things to play with. I know you are in a hurry to go out! They don't mean it. Be realistic about their distraction levels and talk to them at eye level or, alternatively, bring the shoes to them. If you need to hurry in the morning, be ultra-organised, with clothes left out the night before. Shouting across a room won't help to move these children in the right direction.

Make sure you give butterfly children plenty of playmates, imaginative play opportunities, nature outings and craft, as well as daydreaming time. We need butterfly children in this world. As adults, sanguine types will bring colour, joy and positivity to our lives, even though they may remain a little unreliable and forgetful at times!

Parenting Tip:

Don't expect sanguines to be settled for more than half an hour, and I'll repeat: give them the freedom of time.

Gift:

These children bring magic into life with a surprise flower or a fairy house made of twigs in the garden.

Extra note:

Children aged from toddler to ten are predominantly in a sanguine stage.

Choleric

Attributes of the choleric temperament include forceful, active, aggressive at times, individual, natural leaders and surplus energy. The colour associated with the temperament is red and the element is fire. The adult body type is short and stocky (with wide, muscular shoulders). They tend to walk heel down, with a sure step. They also tend to be socially orientated, looking outward to the world – often with the intention of making a difference.

The positive side of the choleric temperament is will in action; cholerics have a total preoccupation with a job until it is done. Cholerics are competent and confident characters. Reliable and dependable, cheerful and optimistic, anxious to do well and to please others. There is no such word as 'can't' in their vocabulary: challenge them and they will go out of their way! They are good-hearted and generous. Show appreciation for their efforts and they are very loyal.

At times, they can be brusque and off-hand, aggressive and loud. Be aware, they are intelligent and sensitive. If overly criticised they will feel defeated and become depressed, with a tendency to whine or complain until they can shake it off, rising up again to the next challenge. Born entrepreneurs, they like to be the boss: 'My way or the highway!' What is the personal life lesson they are learning? Self-control.

Choleric Children – Fiery Children

A choleric child is often the first one other parents notice at playgroup! Fiery, strong-willed, active, impulsive – these children require activity, challenges, tasks and responsibilities, outside play, long bike rides and bush walks. They want to be active and useful. Boredom leads to destructive behaviour – they need to be physical.

Add fire to fire and we all go up in flames. In challenging situations, guide them out of the heat of the moment, and talk afterwards. Inspire them with stories, explain natural consequences to actions and demonstrate how to lead! Learning self-regulation and control is the key to a positive and balanced development of the choleric type. These fiery, strong-willed children need to look up to you – model something that you are good at and passionate about (scuba-diving, kicking a goal, knitting). If not guided, cholerics have a tendency to use their hands and strength instead of words. Fiery children need a challenge in difficult moments. 'I bet you can't get your pyjamas on before I finish the washing up!' They require adults who are calm and assertive; initially they will push you, and then settle down when they feel your inner resolve.

While still needing strong boundaries and the art of listening, direct eye-to-eye confrontation rarely helps a situation with a choleric. Diffuse the energy firmly, and chat later while you're washing up together. An explanation of the outcomes of their behaviour is helpful, so long as it's delivered in a non-confrontational way. Each action creates a reaction; guide the choleric child to understand this and to make the right choices.

Parenting Tips:

Praise rather than blame. Are there traits you wish to see again? Catch them doing the right thing and praise! Inspire their leadership qualities: true leaders look after others. 'Clever hands are useful for helping not hitting.' Cholerics are not looking for trouble but for challenges. Hold them in a space where their bountiful energy is channelled in positive ways. Contain the fire – don't douse it.

Gift:

Even though today they may be demanding, bossy and at times aggressive, choleric characters are the leaders and inventors of tomorrow!

Extra notes:

Toddlers (and teenagers) are predominantly in a choleric stage.

Melancholic

Melancholic characters are quite reserved; their main complaint is feeling misunderstood – the weight of the world is on their shoulders. You may say they are never happy; they are under the influence of gravity, overwhelmed by life's troubles. The melancholic colour is blue and the element is earth. The body type is tall and wired, with a small head, which they tend to hold to one side. They walk with a slight stoop, weighed down by gravity. Their focus is inward and on their troubles. Melancholics are introverts – aloneness is not loneliness to them – in fact they need it to regroup.

They approach situations with extreme caution. This type only requires one or two friends to feel socially abundant. Don't try and cheer them up or jolly them along. They can be self-opinionated and believe they are always right, but if you persist with your ideas and point of view, they will be flattered and cooperate.

Their compassionate nature flows if anyone is in trouble or requires advice. A burdened situation is not scary to them – they are comfortable with pain.

Melancholic Children – Worrier Children

The worrier children seem at odds with the stereotypical view of childhood as effervescent and carefree. They are more likely to be quiet and reserved, often playing alone or with one friend. They love routine and are unsettled by change – they'll want the same thing for lunch for six years.

With the worrier type, under no circumstances try to change their nature or toughen them up! To make these children strong, hold them close, do not push them away. To ease their fears, allow them to express them, don't override them. These sensitive types require strong and committed love and acceptance. They often love warm, not cold, food, and the warmth of love and compassion.

Encourage melancholics to feel safe in the world: gently teach bravery and step out holding hands. Understand when to encourage (and, at times, insist) on an outing or adventure, letting them know 'We will try, and if you don't like it, after a short time we will leave.'

When they hurt their knee, tell a sorrowful tale of when you cut your knee as a child. They will be listening!

Parenting Tip:

Understand that melancholic children feel rich with one good friend, not in large social situations. They plan for a rainy day (three torches on the bedside table in case of a power cut). Be firm, creative to move beyond their fears, but don't override them.

Gift:

Given the right environment, worrier children will become compassionate advocates for the poor and sick in the future.

Extra notes:

Life, and change, is difficult in their own mind. The middle-age stage of life is a general melancholic stage.

Phlegmatic

The phlegmatic temperament is also introverted. Think of a calm sea, but include the currents underneath! Often misunderstood as uninteresting, featureless and unexciting, they have hidden depths. With a patient nature, they can be unruffled, unperturbed and calm – loving a quiet and tranquil atmosphere. The phlegmatic colour is green and the element is water. The body type is short and round, with a tendency to put on weight. Their walk has a slow and consistent rhythm. They never get bored of their own company. Introverted in nature, they do not like to stand out in a crowd.

An intense inner life (the hidden currents) and ability to

maintain inner harmony are the positive traits of a phlegmatic character. They can be witty, amusing and good listeners; they are great with advice.

They will check bills and reconcile statements. They absorb information slowly and require time to think. They prefer repetitive work rather than leadership roles, and will complete it with care and precision (if they haven't opened a book). Start a book and the phlegmatic won't stop until the last page is finished.

See their eyes light up with the mention of food! Food and drink is a sacred ritual for them, which can get out of balance.

Rudolf Steiner said this temperament makes the best teachers.

If pushed, they can act in a choleric manner! Ask how they have been and the answer will be 'Fine'; ask what they have been doing and the answer will be 'Nothing much'. A tendency to idleness and inactivity requires monitoring. As adults they require the strength to self-direct, and must find the will to move off the sofa.

Phlegmatic Children – Calm Children

These children sit quietly as babies, and tend to be compliant toddlers. They do not need stimulating entertainment, lots of activities or friends. Allow them their deep, quiet life. They bring stability. Get to know them one-on-one to discover their inner life and humour.

The compliant child must not be underestimated or ignored. Acknowledge, acknowledge, acknowledge.

Parenting Tip:

Don't bribe them with food! Create a fun baking session once a week. Be interested in their life. Make sure your home life has quiet and calm spaces, where the phlegmatic child can feel at peace.

Gift:

These easygoing children will become the stable and enduring peace warriors that the earth needs, steady even in difficult times.

Extra note:

The baby stage is a phlegmatic stage.

Ages and Stages

The baby stage of life, from conception until the baby becomes a toddler, is a phlegmatic stage. Peace and quiet, warmth and a loving atmosphere, tranquillity, bonding, breast milk and natural baby foods are required.

The toddler stage is – yes, you've guessed – choleric! Creative discipline is important, as well as time to complete new skills, to help with home tasks, and to be mobile and active. Play, play!

From toddler to age ten, the child is in the sanguine stage. All the ideas in *Happy Child, Happy Home* add the magic three 'C's (Connection, Creativity and Communication) that children thrive on.

Adolescents are, once again, in a choleric stage. Choose your battles, use humour and talk reasonably. This is a good age for community work and travel.

Middle-age brings melancholy. It is characterised by inward thoughts and an increase in worry (possible mid-life crisis and nostalgic memories).

Finally, old age returns once again, as in the beginning, to a phlegmatic stage. The elderly require peace and quiet, happy solitude and a slow, good life (retirement).

The ability to understand and accept different character types (temperaments) is a useful parenting tool and is also a helpful life skill. It can lead to a greater understanding of our bosses, parents-in-law, even the local shopkeeper!

One can develop the exercise of looking upon the lives of one's fellows and the expressions of their character with the eyes of their angels – with that trusting glance directed to what is in the process of becoming. Understanding temperaments assists us in moving towards a future in which every human being sees a hidden divine essence in every other human being. This is at the centre of what I draw from Rudolf Steiner's teaching.

Reflection

Everyone is the same, only different

Recommended Reading

This is a deep topic, and further recommended reading includes Marieke Anschutz, *Children and their Temperaments* (Floris Books), and Gilbert Childs, *Understanding Your Temperament!* (Sophia Books).

Real Life Story
Karen – Considering the Temperaments of Parents

I found it illuminating to consider the Four Temperaments as parenting styles: to imagine the gifts brought by each parenting temperament, and the areas we need to watch.

Sanguine parents make great story tellers, and bring magic, colour, playfulness, spontaneity and laughter to children. But they may need reminding to focus on children during social situations and to be punctual for children's events!

Choleric parents are good role models, and have boundless energy to run after toddlers. They often take on responsibilities like organising and leading the school fundraising events, and are an active force in their children's lives. Choleric parents have to watch for fiery episodes in themselves; a heated child and parent together will create a bonfire! Also, they must stop and reflect to understand their children with different temperaments – maybe their children are quieter in nature.

Melancholic parents are wonderfully compassionate when children fall over, and they have everything planned for rainy day situations. They may need to watch whether they are overly worrisome and anxious.

Phlegmatic parents bake and cook with great enjoyment and create cosy and calm home environments. Sometimes they need a push to get off the couch and take children outside and on adventures!

Checklist – The Four Temperaments

1. Ponder your different family members' characteristics.

2. Understand the stages of individual temperament development; a child's temperament will be clear by the age of 21.

3. Life itself is a set of temperament stages; understanding these stages helps.

4. Sanguines require focusing and grounding so they can fly and land like butterflies.

5. Cholerics are very useful in getting a job done. Can they work with others without too much heat?

6. Meloncholics feel emotions deeply; they will be a shoulder to cry on.

7. Phlegmatics are stable and peaceful. Everyone needs a phlegmatic friend!

8. Use temperaments as a loose guide. Don't box anyone in.

Chapter Eleven
Happy Child, Happy Earth

Be the change you wish to see in the world.

ARUN GHANDI DESCRIBING MAHATMA GHANDI

Sustainable Family Living

As parents, we need to ask the question: 'What legacy are we leaving for our children?' Can companies and governments clear old-growth rainforest, dredge the seas of life and pump toxic waste into our waterways? No! There is the slow realisation that having a living eco-system that is healthy for all its inhabitants – including the furry, winged and finned kind – is more important than mass profit, or, in one word, greed. Choices today require ethical judgement. This is the century to turn things around, to become a 'green warrior'!

What is turning green? Think of it as like the traffic light system: green means 'go' for the planet. The Earth can continue to be a wonderful place for the next generation to call home. Would we knowingly destroy our own house? Of course not, so why do we stand back and watch our larger home being destroyed? The technological changes that have happened over time are amazing. It would be wonderful, too, if this period in history was the time we turned environmental destruction around – an era in which we learnt to respect Earth: happy child, happy Earth.

To teach our children to respect the Earth's resources, we need to do so ourselves. We are their first role models. This journey to greener lands can happen together, as a family. I am not talking about drastic changes. We do not have to spend a fortune on solar panels or protest along the streets with banners (but please do so, if inclined!). The 101 suggestions for being a green household that are outlined here reflect just a slight change in consciousness: a growing awareness of the preciousness of the Earth.

Happy child, happy Earth

Going green together can help our relationships with each other: I have noticed that many of the following tips lead to a more connected and loving family life. Teaching respect for the planet is a fundamental life skill. Respect for the Earth leads to respect for all the Earth's inhabitants, humans included! As parents of young children, it is our responsibility to cultivate the soil (the soul) – of our children's beautiful hearts and minds – and plant the seeds (the beautiful intentions) that lead to the next generation of champion respect-ers.

Parenting, raising the next generation with awareness, is the most important work in the world. We are helping life evolve. I like the challenge set forth in this statement by Bob Hawke (Australian prime minister, 1983–91) in an interview with Andrew Denton:

> I think we have done the left side of the brain for a long time; we have developed the intellect, logic, technology. It is time now in this era to recognise the importance of the right side of the brain; the qualities of creativity, love and compassion.

The Dalai Lama says,

> Modern education is premised strongly on materialistic values. It is vital that when educating our children's brains we do not neglect to educate their hearts, a key element of which has to be the nurturing of our compassionate nature.

We have the power to teach our young children to love the Earth and, in doing so, to respect our relationships and ourselves. Small changes can be significant. Have you heard the hundredth monkey story? A monkey on an island decided that it would take the potato it found in the ground to the sea's edge and wash it. Soon the other monkeys on the island followed this new idea, and they all had a new food source! When the hundredth monkey washed its potato, a monkey on a neighbouring island got an idea, 'How about I wash this dirty potato at the sea's edge before eating it!' And so the idea went on its way, from island to island.

Let us wash the dirt off our Earth gently and lovingly, and may our ideas for a simple, respectful home life spread across the globe.

The Wonder of Water

Water consciousness is important everywhere, but it's vital if you live in a dry part of the world. Explain to young children that clouds give rain as a special gift. We catch some and save it, to use as our water. Let us respect the clouds and their gift to us by using water wisely. Say, 'Thank you clouds!' as we hop into the bath, or turn on a tap. When it rains say, 'Thank you rain clouds for filling up our water supplies!'

Bath together: save water and have fun! Run a shallow bath for children, and it is not necessary to bath or shower children every day, once they are out of nappies. (Do a spot wash at times too.)

Add a couple of drops of lavender oil to warm water in a bowl: this is a lovely way to wash hands and face before bedtime, helping to create soothing dreams, and leaving more water for the planet!

Use environmentally friendly washing-up liquid. Have fun with water and bubbles without polluting our waterways; this is kind to our children, our dishes and the Earth. Young children love to help with the dishes.

Install dual-flush toilets and teach young children which button to push for what. When toilet training, stick a gold star on the half-flush button. Press to lower the water bill. If you do not have a dual-flush toilet, fill a large plastic bottle with water, and place it in your cistern tank. Put in more bottles if desired. A full flush is 12 l (2½ gal) of water, compared to a small flush of 3 l (½ a gal). That's a big difference! When we're not expecting visitors, do we need to flush each time? Put the lid down and wait until next time: this could save half your toilet water usage.

Change to water-efficient showerheads. One new style of showerhead saves 11,000 l (2420 gal) a year. Have a fun timer in the shower: four minutes only – time's up at the buzz! In the summer months, place a bucket under the shower to collect the water. Carry it out to water the garden or wash a bike.

Only fill the kettle with the water you need. Put leftover water from drink bottles or drained vegetables on the plants!

Use chemical-free shampoos, conditioners, washing powder, toilet cleaners – basically anything that goes into our waterways. Avoid agrichemicals accumulating and creating dire results in our water systems. Keep it clean!

Install a water tank and grow veggies.

Turn taps off while cleaning teeth. Use a special little cup to rinse your mouth, and to wash the brush at the end. A tap running while cleaning teeth, wastes 9 l (2 gal) of water per minute!

Fix dripping taps; in the meantime place a bowl underneath the leaky tap and use it to water the plants.

Are our clothes really dirty? Only wash dirty clothes, not just those wrinkled from one day's use! Wait to wash until you have enough to fill the machine. Wash, where possible, on the cold water wash.

Contemplate the many countries where people (usually women and children) walk 10 km (6 miles) a day for their water supply, and carry it back on their heads! Hold gratitude for the gift of running water.

Visit the nearest reservoir with your children to see how rainwater is stored. This can be a wake-up call if the water level is low.

Wash the car with a bucket; children love to help, and to wash their bikes too. Even better if it is a recycled bucket of bath water. Or, use the local car wash if it recycles the water.

For better absorption into the soil, water the garden – with your tank or recycled water where possible – early in the morning or late in the evening. For water retention, put down pea straw to mulch the garden: it really works!

Rainy days are lovely days. Free water fun: playing in puddles in gumboots, dancing in the rain with umbrellas! Celebrate a rainy day by playing with raindrops.

Drink plenty of water – our bodies love it. Save water everywhere else!

Don't bother monitoring others: what is my water footprint?

Shower each other with love!

If buying a new electrical water appliance, like a dishwasher or washing machine, look for the water saving logo.

Avoid using a half-full appliance.

Watch the water bill and usage go down, and share the positive changes as a family.

Celebrate water in its natural forms on Earth: swim in the sea and rivers, hire a paddle boat, visit a waterfall. Experience the glory of natural water features. Appreciating and wondering about Earth's water kingdom means we won't pollute it, dry it up or spoil it!

Tell children the story of how litter travels the long journey to the sea: down the drains! Teach children to put litter in bins, and to avoid packaged fast food, as so much litter consists of this. Take a rubbish bag on a local walk, especially along a beach or river, and pick up the litter. We may well save a bird's life!

The Treasures of Earth

The Earth – helped by her two friends, warm sunshine and tickling rain – grows the food that we eat. The Earth looks after us and we look after her. The Earth is our home and holds treasures of life: plants, insects and animals. Our own garden is a wonderful and amazing place.

Plant a vegetable garden! This can be a small patch or a large plot, or even a pot on a veranda or balcony. Mix compost through the soil, plant seedlings, water and cover with pea straw. Let children help with their own small wheelbarrow, watering can and shovel. They can experience the wonder of growing food. Plant bulbs, herbs and strawberries in pots. Water carefully and watch what happens…

Plant trees and shrubs that are native to your area in the garden: this will feed local wildlife and save water.

Plant some trees together as a family – fruit trees are always fun! A single tree absorbs one ton of carbon dioxide over a lifetime. If you are renting, buy miniature fruit trees for pots. Observe the four seasons of a fruit tree.

Wonderful children's books celebrate the earth's riches and cycles; keep a lookout for the messages in stories.

Choose places of natural beauty for day trips and holidays. An appreciation of nature creates a greater consciousness of the Earth. Go camping, relax on a picnic rug under a tree, look for four-leaf clovers on a grassy patch, stare up at the stars at night, realise we are all important parts of this big, beautiful universe!

Say a blessing to thank the Earth before mealtimes. Celebrate nature in your home with a seasonal table.

Feed children fresh food. Let them know that food comes from the Earth, not a package, tin or jar. Offer children two pieces of fruit each day and three or more vegetables lightly steamed or chopped fresh.

Compost vegetable scraps. Keep chickens, they eat compost! Buy a worm farm to use up vegetable scraps, or put the worms into the garden. The Earth loves worms. (And children do too!)

Buy a bug-catcher for children to watch the wonderful world of insects. (Remember to let them go afterwards!) Spend time in the garden each day, to see the magic of the natural world.

Explain where packaging goes: deep into the Earth's tummy! Recycle where possible (learn the recycling plastic number system, check with the local council which numbers they accept) and teach children which bin to use. Recycle more: we can save over 1,000 kg (2,200 lb) of carbon dioxide per year by recycling just half of our household waste.

Limit packaging; buy fresh foods. With every food item ask, 'Is this ethical packaging?' and 'Is there another option?' You can save over 500 kg (1,100 lb) of carbon dioxide a year by cutting household garbage down by ten per cent. Understand that packaging does not just disappear. It takes energy and toxins to make and ends up in landfill or in our water ways!

Refrain from using plastic bags; keep recycled bags in the back of the car. Why put fruit and vegetables in plastic bags? (Ok, cherries, maybe.) Make sure children have a little shopping basket too! A plastic bag takes 500 years to decompose and can kill. In the sea, turtles and birds think they are jellyfish and eat them. This is becoming a huge problem. Six billion plastic bags are used in Australia every year. That is 300 per person. What is your country's tally? Chart your own usage for one year. If you do pick up a plastic bag, try to re-use it as a rubbish (or doggie poo) bag.

Baking cakes and biscuits means less packaging and saves money! Make fresh baby food: it needs no jars or processing and it's very healthy for baby.

Try the naked lunch box idea: no wrappers at all. Fresh fruit and vegetables come without wrappers! Avoid cling wrap; cover a bowl with a plate in the fridge.

Can you use things again? Glass jars make great storage jars. Use cardboard from cereal boxes for craft templates.

Phone the customer service telephone numbers of big food and paper companies and ask, 'When will you be using recyclable or biodegradable packaging or goods?'

Recycle boxes into hours of playful fun: trains, boats, cradles and letterboxes.

Can we use other people's rubbish? Go treasure hunting through hard rubbish collections – kids love this! Give away your unused goods to charity bins. If it's broken, can it be fixed?

Children who wear hand-me-downs and passed-on clothing (vintage is in!) are usually able to play in mud and get wonderfully and imaginatively dirty. This is healthy play. Their clothes do not cost the Earth!

Hold a recycled birthday party! Think of fun ways to wrap presents: coloured newspaper, old pieces of fabric and ribbon. Make party decorations. Flags can be made out of old clothes and fabrics. Make your own treats, popcorn and fruit ice lollies – no wrappers!

Have fun making greeting cards and support card companies that use recycled materials.

Pass on toys – wooden ones last from one generation to the next. Buy ethically-sourced wooden and fabric toys where possible, or find imaginative toys in charity shops. Fix broken toys with glue. Mend torn clothes with a needle. Treasure items; they go into landfill if we don't!

Recycle Christmas cards; make them into gift tags for next year. Children love to help with a hole-punch and a piece of wool.

Recycle old envelopes and paper into little writing pads. (These are lovely for a child's pretend café and lists!) Buy recycled paper and office supplies.

Help on local clean-up days – clean up a little area near home, with children helping. And take a rubbish bag while on local walks.

Buy recycled toilet paper. Buy recycled tissues or use a handkerchief.

Use biodegradable nappies and wet wipes. These are also gentler on bottoms and skin rashes as they are chemical-free. Use cut-up old sheets dipped in warm water for comfortable wet wipes! Try a cloth nappy system (if you are inspired), dry pail them using tea tree oil.

Breastfeed where possible: no packaging, bottles, washing or cost!

Use environmentally-friendly and non-toxic baby products – they are kind to baby and our waterways.

Make gifts. Homemade presents by children are precious!

Support the organic industry when buying food and clothing. This ethical industry has no chemicals going into the waterways, soil and air. Yes, it costs more; look on it as an investment in a healthy future. As the organic t-shirt from Target says, 'Good planets are hard to find!'

Remember that processing plastic uses oil and toxins. When discarded, plastic degrades oh so slowly. Buy wisely!

Buy Genetically Modified Free. Keep nature in its natural state, for the health and harmony of people and planet Earth.

Buy good quality crayons and pencils, rather than felt-tip pens: avoid the plastic, and they don't dry up!

Reduce consumption and live simply. As the saying goes, 'The best things in life are free!' For me, life is about loving and connecting with others.

Check labels for chemicals and additives. If they are in our foods, in our air, in our soil and waterways, they are in us!

Take old mobile phones back to phone retailers for recycling. If they are thrown in the rubbish, chemical substances can seep into the landfill and contaminate groundwater and the soil. The same applies to fridges, microwaves, computers and other electrical goods. See your council for help.

What do you need for Christmas? Donate to others.

Let's do our best, within our lifestyles; small changes count.

The Marvel of Energy on Tap

Energy from our plug sockets and light switches is made in factories that put smoke into our air. These factories dig deep into the Earth's belly. Let's use our power wisely and waste little. Special energy can be made from the Sun, the wind, the temperature of the Earth and even the waves! Use these good-for-the-planet power sources if you can.

Turn lights off! This helps the planet and saves money. Do light checks often. 'Can we spot some cheeky lights that are still on?' Turn appliances off at the plug, especially those with standby lights. five per cent of power consumption is merely appliances on standby.

We do not need to have our own solar panels or wind turbines to use alternative power. To make a change, ask suppliers, 'Is there a green energy option?'

Install solar hot water and electricity if you can.

Hang washing on the line (the Sun and wind would love to dry it for us!) or on an indoor drying rack.

Change to energy-efficient compact light bulbs. One light bulb changed saves up to 75 per cent of energy consumption.

Dress warmly: lovely slippers, fluffy dressing gowns, woolly socks and comfy jumpers for winter. Rug up, rather than turn the heating up.

The same applies with air conditioning. Keep it off, use water and cotton clothing to stay cool where possible.

Buy your young children toys free from electrical cords or batteries! These are wonderful for the Earth and for your children's imaginations.

Sing to children – stay connected! Turn off the TV and live your own life. Read a good book in natural sunlight – it uses zero electricity!

Have some home days each week. Leave the car in the drive, connect and slow down at home. Home is where the heart is!

Take car-free walks together in the local area. Carpool when you can. It's fun!

Look for fuels blended with biofuels, such as ethanol – made from sugarcane aka the Sun! Check your car tyres (stay inflated longer!), to ensure your car runs efficiently. Every litre of petrol saved keeps 10 kg (22 lbs) of carbon dioxide out of the environment.

Pedal power rules! Get a baby carrier or child seat for the bicycle. Ride away!

Take public transport. Children love train, tram and bus journeys. Hey, let's look out of the window!

Locate your nearest farmer's market. Follow the 100 km (60 miles) food rule: how far has your food travelled?

Support local businesses.

Eat healthily, in season.

Sustainable Relationships

Love is the greatest energy of all!

Cuddle to keep warm and healthy. Touch on a daily basis!

Make your own fun as a family, play hide-and-seek games together.

Light up the world with a smile!

Warm the world up with your heart.

Encourage children to love the Earth in creative ways.

Support Fair Trade – respect our fellow human beings. Were your products made using ethical labour?

Have a family meeting at a mealtime to talk about simple and effective changes. Think up energy-saving ideas. Physical changes reflect a change in attitude, in conscious thinking, feeling and behaving. What is my family's footprint on the Earth?

Something to Try

Lying on the earth connects you to the Earth. Purchase a new picnic blanket – a family Christmas present. In the summer months go camping. Put the tent up in the garden for summer play (and night) fun!

A Word from a Dad – Michael

Change can happen! Witness cigarette smoking: forty years ago, people smoked anywhere. Today we accept that smoking is acceptable in very few places. Who would have thought this possible back then?

A Word from Seven-year-old Jayson

I never flush the toilet when I do a wee to save water at home. I try to stop myself from having long showers.

Real Life Story
Pat – Sustainable Family Living

Recently I have tried to become more and more conscious of sustainable living practices. What I did not realise as I set out on this endeavour was how much pleasure and joy it would bring to my family life. Being sustainable is fundamentally a caring attitude. The attitude of caring comes from the heart so it brings joy.

At home I try to buy recycled paper goods. I use water wisely, and grow some of my own vegetables. I home-bake most meals, carpool with friends' children to school, and take the time to notice nature.

I gain great pleasure from noticing the Earth and her many faces and seasons. I take holidays in national parks. I have added a walk in nature to my weekly routine. Caring for the Earth is a worthwhile cause in life, and it makes me happier. My own experiences and attitude definitely affect my children, as I role model care for the Earth. It will be their Earth next!

Checklist – Happy Child, Happy Earth

This whole chapter is one long checklist for becoming a sustainable family. Go back, have another look. Tick off some of the points that might work for you; small changes make a big difference!

Epilogue
Childhood Memories

I conclude my Conscious Parenting workshops with the question: 'What is your first childhood memory?' I find the answers fascinating. Memories are made when a strong emotion is present, perhaps surprise, wonder and joy, or negative emotions of fear, anger and sorrow.

Here is a selection of happy memories told by parents reflecting on their own childhoods. Many memories are common to all of us, and children today like the same things! In this fast-paced, technological century, a child still loves to climb a tree or onto Dad's back, to bake with Nan or play a treasure hunt game. It's important to remember this!

By including the ideas below into family life, parents create memories for tomorrow's adults. A powerful thought!

Sharing Childhood Memories:

Family camping trips! On one trip, Dad made a treasure hunt. Once we had found the sweets we had to put them in a tub and then share them out.

Mum invited me into the kitchen to help make a birthday cake. I felt great stirring the mixture and licking the spoon at the end. My first memory is how important I felt when the cake was handed out!

Playing outside, making cubbies: the cubbies were magical for us, like our own home.

The excitement of losing my first tooth!

My dog! How I would stoke him and place my head on his warm belly. My childhood dog was a comfort and a friend for me. He was the best!

My first bike for Christmas, and travelling fast!

My party dress – I remember in particular the joy of dressing up for a party.

The first time the letters of my name made sense.

I loved to watch my grandad in the garden, digging and planting vegetables in rows. It felt special when he gave me a job. I saw how much he cared for his vegetable patch. I particularly liked digging alongside him.

Lying on Dad's stomach listening to his breathing and his stomach making all these different noises. It was incredible to my ears. I remember pulling on a stomach hair, and watching his skin rise. Magic!

The tree in my garden had a low limb and Mum tied a rope as a halter around the trunk, which became my horse. I spent many happy hours riding my pony.

Playing outside on a circle of tree stumps, I would jump from one to the next. In a game, the stumps were a safe space! At times the circle was a boat or castle. One circle of stumps, so many games!

Hopping onto Dad's back and riding him like a horse.

My nan's kitchen, I can vividly see the wallpaper, and smell the baking.

My birthday at kindergarten: the teacher took me to her office and showed me a special cardboard cake. She gave me a magic wand to tap on the cake. She lifted up the cake and a card with guinea pigs was underneath. An incredible piece of magic!

Being outdoors. We lived on a farm and were outdoors a lot.

This list of memories recalls creativity, games involving a child's imagination and moments of connection with adults: the three 'C's (connection, creativity and communication) in action!

Something to Try

Write down happy childhood memories. What are happy memories made of? Ask friends and loved ones for theirs. Remember to do these memory-making activities with your own children.

A Thought from Four-year-old Billy

When someone loves you, the way they say your name is different. You just know that your name is safe in their mouth.

A Word From A Dad – Michael

When we wake up to the fact that we are onto a good thing, parenting is terrific.

A Word from Seven-year-old Jayson

My first memory is of the bird feeder, just watching it and waiting for birds. Also, riding in a toy car into the surgical room for my eye operation, I do not remember the eye operation, but I do remember the toy car.

A Word from my Daughter, Jess, aged Twelve

The first thing I remember is being on holiday in New Zealand. I dropped a stone on my foot. I remember sitting at the table with Dad, and telling him my foot hurt. Ouch! He gave me a cuddle.

I wish that as you read *Happy Child, Happy Home* and implement some of the ideas in everyday family life, new nourishing memories are born in the adults of tomorrow – in our children of today.

Find me at www.skiptomylouparenting.com for a free monthly newsletter with craft, play and Creative Discipline tips, and share the parenting journey ahead...

More on Parenting & Child Health from Floris Books

A Guide to Child Health
A Holistic Approach to Raising Healthy Children
Dr Michaela Glöckler & Dr Wolfgang Goebel

Calm Kids
Help Children Relax with Mindful Activities
Lorraine E. Murray

Children's Creative Play
How Simple Dolls and Toys Help Your Child Develop
Karin Neuschütz

Nurturing Potential in the Kindergarten Years
A Guide for Teachers, Carers and Parents
Cornelius Boogerd

Stress-free Parenting in 12 Steps
Christiane Kutic

Why Children Don't Listen
A Guide for Teachers and Parents
Monika Kiel-Hinrichsen

You and Your Teenager
Understanding the Journey
Jeanne Meijs

Order from **www.florisbooks.co.uk** and get a FREE BOOK when you subscribe to our mailing list.